Praise for
FEHERTY

"Remarkable, and a compelling roller coaster ride about one of my favorite persons. Great book."
—Jay Bilas, ESPN

"John Feinstein's new biography of the golfer and commentator is rich with anecdotes and a glimpse of his darker side.... John Feinstein's entertaining new book, *Feherty*, captures it all—and adds a few more over-the-top tales to the Feherty legend.... Feinstein writes in a book that shows, again, the author's ability to get his subjects to open up."
—*Washington Post*

"Feinstein tells the tale of a middle-tier Irish golf professional who finds success as the resident funnyman on American golf telecasts and then as the surprisingly insightful host of a prime-time interview show on the Golf Channel.... Off-stage, though, he was haunted by sadness. This is a theme that Mr. Feinstein explores with sympathy, aided by Mr. Feherty's own unflinching self-analysis."
—*Wall Street Journal*

"An affectionate portrait of the popular Northern Irish golfer and commentator. Interviewing numerous people in Feherty's orbit as well as the man himself, prolific sportswriter Feinstein profiles his

good friend in an engaging biography. He nimbly chronicles his subject's early years in his usual crisp, polished prose.... Terrific personal anecdotes pepper the text, providing both frivolity and insights into the game."
—*Kirkus Reviews*

"Renowned author John Feinstein has delivered his definitive biography [on Feherty], which will give you a greater appreciation for how he got here.... Feinstein does an excellent job throughout the book of showing how, just when one part of Feherty's life is on the rise, he faces adversity elsewhere."
—*Brooklyn Digest*

"Feinstein is a fantastic storyteller and author and this book is anything but varnished as we learn more about the Feherty story."
—*Fore!Golfers Network*

"*Feherty* is a lighthearted yet poignant story of a man who achieved modest success as a golf pro and then skyrocketed to fame as a commentator and Renaissance man of the world. For both avid and casual fans of the sport, it is an affectionate and entertaining biography.... The book is loaded with anecdotes from Feherty's life. Feinstein is a brilliant writer and reporter, and the stories range from laugh-out-loud funny to moving.... The triumphs and tragedies of his life have been handsomely chronicled by a truly accomplished writer who has produced another in a long line of sports masterpieces. This glorious portrait of a beloved sports figure whose life behind the cameras was a constant struggle is thoughtful, candid, and balanced. You will enjoy reading it."
—*Bookreporter*

FEHERTY

ALSO BY JOHN FEINSTEIN

Raise a Fist, Take a Knee

The Back Roads to March

The First Major

The Legends Club

Where Nobody Knows Your Name

One on One

Moment of Glory

Are You Kidding Me!

Living on the Black

Tales from Q School

Last Dance

Next Man Up

The Classic Palmer

Let Me Tell You a Story

Caddy for Life

The Punch

Open

The Last Amateurs

The Majors

A March to Madness

The First Coming

A Civil War

Winter Games

A Good Walk Spoiled

Play Ball

Running Mates

Hard Courts

Forever's Team

A Season Inside

A Season on the Brink

FEHERTY

The Remarkably Funny and Tragic Journey of Golf's David Feherty

JOHN FEINSTEIN

New York

Hachette Books
Hachette Book Group
1290 Avenue of the Americas
New York, NY 10104
HachetteBooks.com
Twitter.com/HachetteBooks
Instagram.com/HachetteBooks

First Trade Paperback Edition: May 2024

Published by Hachette Books, an imprint of Perseus Books, LLC, a subsidiary of Hachette Book Group, Inc. The Hachette Books name and logo is a trademark of the Hachette Book Group.

The Hachette Speakers Bureau provides a wide range of authors for speaking events. To find out more, go to hachettespeakersbureau.com or email HachetteSpeakers@hbgusa.com.

Books by Hachette Books may be purchased in bulk for business, educational, or promotional use. For information, please contact your local bookseller or Hachette Book Group Special Markets Department at: special.markets@hbgusa.com.

The publisher is not responsible for websites (or their content) that are not owned by the publisher.

Library of Congress Control Number: 2023930986

ISBNs: 978-0-306-83000-6 (hardcover), 978-0-306-83001-3 (trade paperback), 978-0-306-83002-0 (e-book)

Printed in the United States of America

LSC-C

Printing 1, 2024

This is for Dave Kindred, who has been my friend, my colleague, and my mentor for forty-five years.

CONTENTS

FEHERTY

Introduction

I VIVIDLY REMEMBER THE FIRST TIME I had an up-close encounter with David Feherty.

It was in December 1993 in Ponte Vedra, Florida. I was researching *A Good Walk Spoiled* and had convinced John Morris, who was the head of communications for the PGA Tour, to let me sit in on two days of orientation sessions for those who would be rookies on tour in 1994.

I had spent some time in Palm Springs earlier that month at the finals of PGA Tour Qualifying School—the six-day grind that players had to go through in those days to earn full-fledged status on tour for the next year.

One of those playing in the tournament was Feherty, who really didn't belong in the field of 190 wannabes and hopefuls. He was thirty-five and had won five times on the European Tour. He had also been a part of Europe's Ryder Cup team in 1991, the year of the famous/infamous "War by the Shore" on Kiawah Island in South Carolina.

How good a player was Feherty? Good enough to beat three-time major champion Payne Stewart, 2 and 1, in the singles on Sunday in spite of the fact that an officious marshal tried to keep him from reaching the seventeenth tee.

"By the time we finished sixteen, they had pretty much lost control of the crowd," he told me years later. "The security people cleared a path for Payne, which wasn't easy, but did nothing for me. Apparently, it didn't occur to them that he [Payne] might have an opponent. I had to fight my way through to get to the tee. When I started to walk onto the tee, a very large woman pushed me back and said, 'You can't come up here, fella.'

"I had just lost the last two holes and had gone from 4-up to 2-up, and I was on the verge of panicking. I was *not* in a mood to be messed with. Before I could say anything, Payne put an arm around me and said to the woman: 'Ma'am, I understand just how you feel about this asshole, but I really need him up here on the tee with me.'"

Rescued by his opponent, Feherty then hit the 1-iron of his life to a water-guarded green (the hole was playing 243 yards in a howling wind) and then closed out the match by making par. The United States ended up winning 14.5–13.5 when Bernhard Langer famously missed a six-foot putt on the eighteenth green.

Two years later, Feherty returned home from playing in the European Tour's German Open and found his house empty and a note on the kitchen table from his wife, Caroline. It said, "Moved to Dallas."

Caroline Feherty had taken the couple's two sons, Shey (then five) and Rory (who was not quite two), with her.

"I had no choice," Feherty says. "I wanted to be with my boys. So, even though I was pretty sure there was another man involved, I followed her."

Moving to Dallas meant trying to play on the PGA Tour. His five victories in Europe and his status as a Ryder Cupper were worth exactly nothing when it came to gaining status in the United States. The PGA Tour Qualifying School (it was called a school because early on there had been classes the players had to take to prepare to be club pros) comprised three stages to winnow down the field: four rounds at the first stage, four at the second stage, and six at the final stage. Like most players, Feherty had to play all three stages. At that point in his life, he was a very good player, and he cruised through the school. The top 40 players and ties (45 players in all) made it to the tour. Feherty finished T-11 among the 190 players who started the final stage and easily qualified for his card.

And yet, even after getting his card, as far as the tour was concerned, his past accomplishments meant nothing. He was looked at as one of thirty-two tour rookies (thirteen of the qualifiers had been on tour previously), and as a result, he was required to show up for the two-day "orientation" later in December before he could play the tour.

I had never met him, but since Feherty had been part of the European team during that 1991 Ryder Cup and had been far more decorated than any of the other players at the Q-school finals in 1993, I knew who he was.

That is why I recognized him right away when I walked into the back of the meeting room on the first morning of orientation—even though he was stretched across three chairs, sleeping soundly.

At the front of the room, a woman named Andre Kirby, who was known as a "media coach," was explaining to the rookies how to handle the media. Her message was a more sophisticated golf version of the famous Crash Davis speech in *Bull Durham*. Always compliment other players, the golf course, the people running the tournament, the volunteers, the PGA Tour, and, whenever possible, God for giving you the opportunity to play the great game of golf. *Never* criticize anyone and always say you're just hoping to play well tomorrow—or next week—if you happen to be speaking on a Sunday. Always tell your listeners you are planning to give "110 percent."

That has always been one of my favorite jock phrases since it is impossible to give more than 100 percent.

At some point during Kirby's explanation of how to answer questions without ever actually answering a question, Feherty woke up. He put up a hand and said, "Can I ask a question?"

Hearing his Irish accent, Kirby said, "Glad you can join us, Irish. What's your question?"

Still blinking away sleep—not to mention a massive headache—Feherty asked, "Is there something wrong with just telling the truth?"

Immediately, I knew I liked David Feherty.

The first time I actually spoke to Feherty was seven months later, at the 1994 Open Championship, held that year at Turnberry. Here in the United States, "the Open," as the British marketers now call it, is known as "the British Open"—to distinguish it from the US Open, which most Americans call "the Open."

Regardless of what it is called, the tournament is the oldest of golf's four major championships and was first held in 1860—thirty-five years before the first US Open, fifty-six years before the PGA Championship, and seventy-four years before the first Masters.

And while the Masters, sport's greatest tribute to White privilege, is revered in the United States above all golf tournaments, the Open Championship is considered *the* number one golf event by all of Europe and most of the world.

In 1994, Feherty shot a 4-under-par 66 in the third round and trailed the coleaders, Fuzzy Zoeller and Brad Faxon, by two shots. Already well-known in Europe for his smarts and sense of humor, Feherty was brought into the interview room to talk to the media. When he finished, Dave Sheinin and I trailed him out of the tent.

Sheinin and I are now colleagues at the *Washington Post*. Back then, though, he was working at the *Miami Herald*. We introduced ourselves. Feherty looked at Sheinin and said, "*Miami Herald*? Do you know Carl Hiaasen?"

Occasionally, when I say "*Washington Post*," an athlete will ask if I know Bob Woodward and Carl Bernstein—though it doesn't happen often, especially nowadays, fifty-one years after the Watergate break-in. But an athlete who was familiar with humorist Carl Hiaasen and who—apparently—read his syndicated column regularly? To the best of my knowledge that was a first—and, as it turned out, a last.

I was tempted to jump in and say that Hiaasen and I had the same literary agent, but the question hadn't been directed at me. When Sheinin said he didn't know Hiaasen, Feherty expressed disappointment and then said, "Well, if you ever do meet him, you can tell him, I'm a fan—for whatever that's worth."

The next day Feherty shot an even-par 70 to finish T-4, five shots behind Nick Price, who finished eagle-birdie to shoot 66 and win the second of his three major titles. To this day, Feherty wonders if he really *wanted* to win the championship.

"I'm not saying I didn't believe I wanted to win or that I wasn't trying," he said to me almost thirty years after Price's win. "But I had a few putts around the turn that, if I'd made them, I might have had a serious chance to win coming down the stretch. I didn't make any of them. To this day, I wonder if I didn't subconsciously believe,

'I'm not good enough to be an Open champion. I don't deserve to be an Open champion.' It certainly wasn't anything I thought about in the moment. But later, looking back, I'm not so sure I wanted to deal with the responsibility and the attention that would have come with being a major champion. I knew it would be a life-changing event. I'm not so sure I could have handled those changes."

It wasn't as if David was an unknown in those days, with his fifteen years on the European Tour, five wins, and his 1991 Ryder Cup performance. He was as well-liked as anyone on the tour because of his self-deprecating sense of humor and his willingness to share his honest thoughts with the media.

"I've always thought that for most people who are Irish, being funny is a sixth sense," he likes to say. "My dad had it, so did my mom. When I was a kid, humor was my defense mechanism in school. I had ADD, but of course, in those days it was undiagnosed. So, most of the teachers treated me like I was stupid. My response was usually humor. It became a habit."

Feherty always insisted that the most thrilling part of the '91 Ryder Cup wasn't his win over Stewart but being part of a team room in which Seve Ballesteros was the clear-cut leader and cheerleader.

"Every night he would give us all a pep talk," he remembers. "He was like a football coach. He'd walk around the room and tell us *why* we were going to win; *why* we were better than the Americans; *why* there wasn't a thing to worry about or be nervous about.

"He was absolutely great. I always thought he could change the weather with the way he reacted to shots on the golf course. When he missed a key putt—which he didn't do often—his face would turn purple and, almost right away it seemed, the sky would turn black.

"I still remember Saturday night, he stood behind me, massaging my shoulders, telling me I was *better* than Payne, that he'd been watching me all week and he absolutely *knew* I was going to beat him.

"All of that was thrilling. And I remember thinking, 'My God, Seve and I are friends! This is the coolest thing that's ever happened to me.'"

Ballesteros's faith in Feherty paid off with his Sunday victory over Stewart. Feherty's most vivid memory of that afternoon isn't shaking hands with Stewart on the seventeenth green but kneeling behind the eighteenth green, next to Lawrence Levy, a golf photographer, who had been around the sport for more than twenty years.

"We were all kneeling so as not to block the crowd on eighteen when Hale [Irwin] and Bernhard [Langer] walked up with everything on the line. It was so tense it was as if there was no air to breathe. I remember I was shaking like a pregnant nun, and I know I wasn't alone. I think everyone was shaking.

"After Hale missed his par putt, Bernhard had six feet for par. If he made it, the match would be split 14–14 and we'd retain the Cup. If he missed, they won. Taking the Cup home on the Concorde, regardless of score, would be a massive win for us.

"As Bernhard walked up to the putt, Lawrence whispered to me, 'The last German who was under this kind of pressure shot himself in a bunker in Berlin in 1945.'

"I had to clap my hand over my mouth to keep from laughing. It was an awful thing to say, I know that, but at the moment, it struck me as very funny. Lawrence had an off-the-wall sense of humor to say the least."

Langer missed the putt, and the Americans won, causing US captain Dave Stockton to say that the outcome proved that the best golf in the world was being played in the United States. That was, at best, some serious hyperbole.

A week later, Feherty was in Stuttgart and ran into Ballesteros, his new best friend, in the locker room.

"Seve!" he said. "How are you?"

"I'm great, Doug," Ballesteros replied. "How about you?"

So much for being Seve's pal.

He might never have become Seve's pal—I'm not sure Seve had very many pals—but Feherty did become one of the best-liked players anywhere he went to play: Europe, the United States, Asia, and South Africa.

People like David William Feherty. For the record, his first name on his birth certificate is William—the same name as his father—but it wasn't supposed to be that way. William (Billy) Feherty filled out his son's birth certificate wrong in the hospital. "He was drunk," Billy Feherty's second child—and only son—says today. "So, he reversed the names and I ended up being William David legally instead of David William. No one [except for Seve] has ever called me anything but David."

His playing career was cut short by a number of factors: serious elbow issues, serious drinking and drug issues, and a seriously bad first marriage.

William David was rescued by two things: Anita Schneider and CBS Sports.

He had moved to Dallas in 1993 after finding the three-word kitchen table note from Caroline and had tried briefly to rescue the marriage. "I knew it wasn't likely," he says. "But I was willing to try if only because I believed it was the best thing for the boys. She wasn't willing."

By 1995, David was living in a two-bedroom apartment and had informal custody of his two sons most of the time he wasn't on the road and was drowning himself in alcohol and drugs. He had taken to running, "à la Forrest Gump," and his weight had dropped to under 150 pounds. "I looked like I was HIV positive," he says.

In fact, the thought that he was HIV positive crossed Anita Schneider's mind on their first date. She had two sons from a previous marriage and had recently moved from Houston to Dallas. Though Feherty was still going through his divorce, the parallels were obvious. That was why their mutual friend Gary Knott and Anita's friend Jennifer Canavinno thought setting them up on a blind date might be a good idea.

It wasn't.

David showed up drunk. Not long after the foursome had sat down at a table in an Italian restaurant in Highland Park, a Dallas suburb, David took a straw, reached across the table, and drained Anita's drink.

"I was trying to be patient, but that was it," Anita says. "I stood up and said, 'I'm sorry, but I really have to go now.'"

David was drunk, but he still quickly realized he had behaved badly. Plus, even through his alcoholic haze, he liked Anita. "She was pretty, and she had to have a sense of humor to last as long as she did before she finally left," he says. "She gave it about thirty minutes, which was a lot more than I deserved. I was pretty sure I liked her. So, I went to Gary and asked him if he would ask Anita if she would give me one more chance. I knew she would say no—had to say no—but I asked anyway."

He also told Knott to promise Anita that if she was willing to give him one more chance, he would promise to show up sober.

Remarkably, she agreed. "Underneath all the issues, even drunk, I saw a kindness in him," she says. "I'm not exactly sure how I saw it, but I sensed it. I think David's gotten a lot of mulligans in life from people because of that. He can make mistakes, makes them all the time, but there's absolutely no malice in him. Even that first night, I think I knew that, although I really was convinced he was HIV positive."

They decided to go to a Texas Rangers baseball game. Anita wasn't much of a fan but had taken her boys to games, first in Houston and then in Dallas, and David had been to one baseball game—at Fenway Park—when he spent a week in Boston as part of an international trip taken by his high school class. Even though neither one of them knew very much about the sport, it seemed like a pleasant place to spend an evening. David showed up sober—and early. Anita was charmed by how hard he was trying to make up for what had happened on the first date.

"Sometime around the fifth or sixth inning, she stood up and said, 'Would you like a hot dog and a beer?'" he says. "It was the first time in several years that a woman had offered to do something that nice for me. I realized right at that moment that I wanted to marry her. I can't tell you exactly why, but that's how I felt."

David still wasn't divorced, but Anita helped him find a lawyer who was able to finally get the divorce finalized. It wasn't as if David's troubles ended a year later on the day—May 31, 1996—that he and Anita got married, but her presence for the last twenty-seven years has made dealing with them possible. "If it wasn't for her, I'd be dead," he often says. There's not a trace of a smile or any indication that he's joking or exaggerating when he says it.

David and Anita's daughter, Erin, who was born in 1998, agrees with her father. "Honestly, I'm not sure how my mother put up with it at times," she says. "I've watched a lot of what's gone on, more than I wanted to watch or see. I think a lot of times the thing that's brought him back is fear that she'll leave him."

"That's 100 percent true," her father says.

What I have learned in researching this book is that no one I've known has depended on the kindness of others more than David Feherty. The reason so many have been willing to go out of their way to help him is the kindness that Anita sensed in him on that disastrous first date.

"You can say a lot of things about my dad," Rory Feherty says. "And they're all true. But underneath it all, he has a heart of gold."

Everyone who has ever known him has a story about David's generosity. Here's one of mine. In 2005, Tom Watson and I started a golf tournament named after Bruce Edwards, Watson's longtime caddie and close friend who had also been a close friend of mine. I had, in fact, written a book about Bruce and Tom titled *Caddy for Life*, while Bruce was dying of ALS (a.k.a. Lou Gehrig's disease). There were two reasons for founding the event: one was to raise money for ALS research; the other was to keep Bruce alive in the minds and hearts of all of us who had known him.

In 2006, Watson and Feherty had become close friends, in large part because Watson had gone out of his way to help David deal with his alcoholism. By then, David had become a TV star, working for CBS, but he was still fighting a losing battle with his addictions. The first two dinner speakers at the Bruce Edwards Celebrity Golf Classic were Mike Krzyzewski and Dick Vitale. Both were terrific, but neither had known Bruce. In the fall of 2007, I wanted a speaker who had actually known Bruce.

Feherty was a perfect fit. He'd known Bruce well; they had spent many a night drinking together. I asked him if he would come and speak, and he instantly said yes. He told stories about Bruce that brought tears to a lot of eyes. And, not surprisingly, before he was done, he left the audience laughing so hard that some literally fell out of their chairs.

One of those who loved Feherty's talk was Steve Bisciotti, the owner of the Baltimore Ravens. When David finished, Bisciotti said to me, "If you can get him to come and speak in my box to all my friends next season before one of our games, I'll give the charity an extra $50,000."

That was a *lot* of money. I asked Feherty if he'd be willing to do it. "An extra 50K for the charity?" he said. "Of course, I'll do it."

And so, the following September, he flew into Baltimore from Dallas on a Sunday morning and I picked him up at the airport. As we drove to the stadium, I said, "Before I forget, give me your plane ticket receipt so I can have the charity reimburse you for it."

It was the least I could do; he was giving up a Sunday at home with his family to fly round-trip from Dallas to Baltimore and back to entertain Bisciotti's friends in order to help raise serious money for our cause.

Feherty looked at me like I had just landed from the moon. "What are you talking about?" he said. "I can pay for my plane ticket."

"I know that," I said. "But you shouldn't. You're already raising $50,000 for us today. At least let us pay for your plane ticket."

"No," Feherty said firmly. "Now, tell me more about the people I'll be speaking to today."

For the record, Feherty raised more than $50,000 that day because when he was finished, a number of Bisciotti's friends asked me how they could donate to the charity.

The day also produced one of his more memorable lines. Nick Faldo—excuse me, *Sir* Nick Faldo—had become famous for his relationships with women who were considerably younger than he was at that point in his life.

Feherty shook his head sadly that afternoon and said there was bad news within the European Ryder Cup team, which Faldo was scheduled to captain in Louisville the next week. "Turns out Nick is going to have to leave early," he said. "He's going to need to fly home to London to be present at the birth of his next wife."

It took a split second for the group to get the joke. When they did, they laughed so hard and so long I thought we were all going to miss kickoff.

"Was I OK?" David asked me when he finished.

That might have been the funniest thing he said all day. David Feherty is always OK—way beyond OK—but wonders every single day if he will be OK that day or that night. I told David at one point that the hardest thing about researching this book was finding anyone who had anything critical to say about him.

His wife, son, and daughter, who have been through the lowest of low moments with him, admitted there have been times when he made them crazy, but they all circled back to why they love him.

"He was an absent father a lot of the time when I was growing up," Rory Feherty says. "My brother [Shey] and I were back and forth between his house and our mother's house, and he was on the road playing golf or talking about golf a lot. But when I needed him—*really* needed him—he was there. Always there."

One of the questions I asked those I interviewed for this book was to tell me how they would introduce Feherty to an audience that didn't know him. There were many good answers.

The best came from David's longtime friend, mentor, and fellow golfer-turned-commentator Sam Torrance. "I would say, 'Please welcome David Feherty,'" he says. "'The funniest and kindest person I've ever met.'"

His voice catches as he says it. I hope that by the time you finish this book you will understand why.

CHAPTER ONE

Early Days

T HERE HAS ALWAYS BEEN DEBATE about when "the Troubles" began in Northern Ireland. While they are generally labeled by outsiders as thirty years of tension between Catholics and Protestants, they were more about politics than religion.

For years, there has been a divide in Northern Ireland over the issue of whether the country should remain a part of the United Kingdom or break those ties and become part of a united Ireland. Even today, it is a difficult question and was one of the reasons why Rory McIlroy, who grew up in Holywood, Northern Ireland, was reluctant to take part in the Olympics when golf returned to the Games in 2016. He wasn't certain if he wanted to represent Great Britain or Ireland.

"In the end, regardless of my choice, I'm going to piss somebody off," McIlroy said in 2016. He ended up not taking part in the Olympics that year, using the presence of the Zika virus in Brazil—as many players did—as a reason not to play. He did play in Tokyo in 2021 and represented Ireland.

McIlroy is Catholic, and long before he was born in 1989, most Catholics from Northern Ireland believed that the country should break away from the United Kingdom and formally become part of Ireland. Most Protestants—many of them from Ulster and descendants of those who migrated to Ireland from Scotland, Wales, and England centuries ago—wanted the country to continue to be part of the United Kingdom.

Most people will tell you that the Troubles formally began on August 14, 1969, when British troops were sent into Belfast to quell violence between Catholics and Protestants. David Feherty had turned eleven the day before, having been born on August 13, 1958. He and his family lived in Bangor County Down, a suburb twelve miles east of Belfast.

Feherty grew up Protestant; his family went to the Sixth Bangor Church of Ireland three days a week. David liked church for one reason: the singing. Both his parents sang in the church choir and David joined them when he was six and was labeled "gifted" almost from the start.

His parents, William (Billy) and Violet (Vi) Feherty had three children: David and two daughters—Helen, who is three years older than David, and Deborah, who is eighteen months younger. They lived in a 1,200-square-foot, three-bedroom house at 22 Hazelden Avenue. Helen had her own bedroom; David and Deborah shared a room. "She used to grind her teeth and snore," David remembers. "Made me crazy, so I'd wake her up and tell her to quit it—as if she could control it."

The Feherty's neighbors—at 20 Hazelden Avenue—were the Parsons family, who were Roman Catholics. Mr. Parsons was David's first piano teacher. It never occurred to him that the Parsons were supposed to be the enemy.

"We were very aware of what was going on," Feherty says. "You couldn't *not* be aware. There were identity checks and roadblocks in different places all the time. It became a part of your life to get stopped or to be told, 'You can't go there.' I knew it wasn't normal, that the life we were living wasn't the way it was supposed to be or the way you'd want it to be. But that way of life became normal to us. You just sort of took for granted that this was the way life was— or at least the way *our* life was.

"I remember watching the movie *Belfast*, and all these memories flooded back to me. I said, 'That's my life, that was my boyhood.'"

Belfast, which came out in 2021, is Kenneth Branagh's autobiographical film about his life in Belfast after the Troubles began. Branagh was nine on the day the British troops first showed up, and the film is full of moments that echo with the truth of Feherty's line about life simply not being normal. Branagh's father had a job in London and there were times when the simple act of returning to Belfast became a nightmare. The family eventually moved to London, escaping the violence and bloodshed but leaving their home behind.

Branagh, who had been nominated eight times previously without winning, won the Academy Award for best screenplay for the film.

Unlike Branagh's family and the semifictional family in *Belfast*, Feherty's family stayed. "We were never right in the middle of the worst of it," he says. "It was always there, but there were plenty of places where there was much more violence than where we lived. My dad worked on the docks in Belfast, and that was scary at times. But my mom refused to let it dominate our lives or our thoughts."

Billy Feherty worked for a company called Ulster Ferry, which was a container freight company. David remembers spending a good deal of time at the Belfast docks as a boy, although there was no place in Belfast considered completely safe once the Troubles began.

His mother, who—unlike his father—finished high school, became a personal secretary to a woman who was a member of the British aristocracy. Her name was Edith Vane-Tempest-Stewart, Marchioness of Londonderry. The name sounds as if it comes from *Downton Abbey*, but it's real. "In those days, my mom could type one hundred words a minute on an old Remington," her son remembers. Later, she became a hospital administrator.

David's memories of his boyhood are much like those of Buddy, the nine-year-old portrayed in Branagh's film. The Troubles were ever-present and David realized as he grew up that there were people who thought it was somehow wrong that their Catholic neighbors continued to live on Hazelden Avenue.

There are a number of scenes in *Belfast* that hit right at the heart of Feherty's feelings about those times. Early on, when Buddy asks his dad what is going on in the streets, his father says, "It's all about bloody religion, that's the problem."

"Why then," Buddy asks, "do we go to church?"

Feherty, who now calls himself an agnostic, wonders about that to this day.

Later, Buddy is doing his math homework (known as "maths" in Great Britain) with the help of his grandfather, and Buddy points out to him, "In maths, there's only one right answer."

"If there was only one right answer," his grandfather replies, "people wouldn't be blowing each other up all over this town."

As Buddy and his family prepare to leave Belfast, he goes to see Catherine, the classmate he's had a crush on throughout the film, one last time. After he hands her flowers, he asks his father if perhaps they might be married someday. When his father says that's possible, Buddy says, "But she's a Catholic."

To which his father says, "If she's kind and fair and you two respect each other, she's welcome in our house anytime."

"If only," Feherty says now, "it had all been that simple."

The end of the film is heartbreaking. As Buddy's family—mother, father, and older brother Jack—leaves Belfast, forced to leave Buddy's grandmother (played by Dame Judi Dench) behind, a final tribute to those who lived through the Troubles appears on the screen: "For the ones who stayed. . . . For the ones who left. . . . And for all the ones who were lost."

It is an apt summation of the Troubles and of the way Feherty grew up.

His best subjects in school were English and music, but he was truly gifted in music. As a boy, he sang, played the piano, and played the clarinet. "I really wasn't any good on the piano or the clarinet, but I did have a good singing voice," he says. "Plus, I enjoyed it. I liked to perform."

By the time he was eight, Brian Hunter, the church choir director, was giving him solos like "Once in Royal David's City" and "Christmas Time." Mr. Hunter was also David's music teacher at school, and it was in that class that he stood out.

His English teacher was Jack Murphy, who, unlike other teachers, saw something in David. "He taught me how to use my imagination, and he taught me how to listen," Feherty says. "I think using my imagination helped me a great deal when I started to write. Listening helped make me a better interviewer."

His other teachers weren't as patient with him. David believes he was a classic undiagnosed ADD kid: bright but often unable to focus. Frequently, teachers became impatient with him because they assumed he just didn't want to listen. His classmates often made fun of him because most of his teachers decided he just wasn't very smart or was simply unwilling to listen in class. Or both.

"It gave me an inferiority complex, there's no doubt about that," he says. "That's something I've carried with me my entire life. But it also probably helped me become successful because I wanted to prove people wrong. To some degree, I'm probably still doing that."

His mother never accepted the notion that he wasn't smart or, later, that he had ADD. "To her ADD is an acronym for stupid," he says. "The fact is, I was just bored a lot."

When his voice began to change, Mr. Hunter sent him to get singing lessons from a woman named Karys Denton to help him train to be a tenor. "She was a very stern Polish lady," Feherty remembers. "She would push a grand piano up against the wall and then tell me to push it away from the wall with my stomach in order to strengthen my diaphragm. It was great fun."

The exercise *did* strengthen his diaphragm.

"Generally speaking, I was worthless at school," he says. "Because of the ADD, which was in fact quite real, I couldn't concentrate or didn't concentrate on anything unless it really interested me. I was interested in English because of Mr. Murphy and in music. The rest, I couldn't have cared less about. Most of the teachers didn't help by making me feel like I was stupid. I learned to tune them out most of the time at an early age. Except for Mr. Hunter and Mr. Murphy, I was never a teacher's pet—to put it mildly."

He didn't necessarily shine as an athlete, but he loved sports. His uncle Jack, two years older than his father, had two sons, Brian and Peter, who introduced David to soccer and rugby. By the time he was ten, he was going to the golf course on weekends to caddie for his father.

The Fehertys lived near Bangor Golf Club—two hundred yards from the tenth tee to be precise. Billy Feherty was part of a regular foursome that played every Saturday and Sunday. It was on the golf course that David first realized just how funny his father could be.

One Saturday morning, Billy Feherty asked a member of his foursome, Dr. Des Duignan, if he could prescribe a sleeping pill for him because he'd been having trouble sleeping for several nights. Dr. Duignan wasn't eager to give his friend a sleeping pill, so he began asking him what methods he had used in attempting to fall asleep.

When Billy Feherty finished telling him what he'd been doing, Dr. Duignan said: "Try this tonight: Close your eyes and imagine you're on the first tee here in the morning. Feel the breeze, smell the grass, imagine the sights and sounds that you enjoy when you're on the golf course. Then, start playing your round in your mind's eye. Just imagine hitting good shots and making putts and I guarantee you, you'll be asleep by the turn."

The next morning, Dr. Duignan asked Billy Feherty how he had slept.

"Not good," Billy answered, "but I played very well."

"Did you do what I told you to do?" the doctor asked.

"I did, exactly as you described," Billy said.

"What happened?"

"I shut my eyes and smelled the grass and felt the breeze, just like you said. Then, I started to play. First two holes I made birdie. Third hole I hit my tee shot into a divot, got it out of there to the front of the green. From there, I made the longest putt of my entire life.

Went to the fourth tee three-under-par and hit my tee shot way right. I then spent the rest of the night looking for that damn ball. Never found it. Never slept."

Dr. Duignan gave Billy a prescription at the end of the round.

"My mom had kind of a stoic sense of humor," Feherty says. "Mom would put dinner on the table every night at six o'clock. If my dad was there, fine. If my dad wasn't there, also fine. He would often come home late after time at the pub and would come upstairs to kiss all of us goodnight. You could feel the whiskers on his face and smell the whiskey on his breath.

"One night he came home while we were all still awake. He walked in and said, 'Is my dinner still warm?'

"My mom said, 'It certainly is. It's in the dog's stomach.'"

Vi Feherty credits her husband for David's storytelling ability. "David wasn't that funny when he was young," she says. "Always well-spoken and with a quick wit. But I think the storytelling came from listening to his father. Billy was a wonderful storyteller."

Humor was ever-present in the Feherty household, and it was often needed. Soon after the Troubles started, Billy Feherty was laid off from his job at Ulster Ferry. He started his own small container company and made enough to get by—just barely. His office was located near the docks in the Belfast Telegraph building and one day the building was blown up. It wasn't as easy to get in touch with people in those days, so there was a time when Vi Feherty and her children wondered if Billy was safe.

"We worried, but we didn't worry *that* much," Feherty says. "A lot of the bombings were carried out by protection rackets—some Catholic, some Protestant. They wanted to let people know that as long as they paid them once a month, they'd be safe. More often than not, there was a warning prior to a bomb going off—not always, but a lot of the time. The point wasn't so much to kill people as to scare them.

"There were actually times when people would spectate when the warning came early enough. They'd stand around and say, 'Oh, that was a good one.' It was a way of life, but there were times, tragically, when it was a way of death."

Not long after Billy Feherty had started his own company, his older brother Jack was laid off by British European Airways when the airline merged with what was then BOAC—British Overseas Airways Corporation—to form British Airways. It was at that point, in 1974, that the two brothers started a travel agency, which actually had a good deal of success.

"It was a different time," David says. "It wasn't as if they got rich, but they did well enough to get by. Dad and my uncle Jack used to deliver tickets to customers in person at their homes. Dad was always gregarious and outgoing. He never met someone who wasn't a friend. Jack was quieter, so Dad did most of the deliveries. For him, the notion of going to people's doors and delivering tickets to them came very naturally."

Feherty Travel still exists today. When Billy decided to retire, he chose to sell to Raymond Parker, who had been a loyal employee since university—the only job he's ever had—and who has carried on the legacy and tradition Billy instilled.

CHAPTER TWO

Following the Dream

NOT SURPRISINGLY, DAVID FELL IN love with golf while caddying for his father and learning to understand the camaraderie of the sport. His father had cut some clubs down for him when he was very young, and as he grew, he began sneaking onto the course at Bangor Golf Club more and more often. "I'd almost always get caught and thrown off," he says. "But I'd usually get to play a few holes before that happened. I did the same thing on the range. I'd sneak on, hit some balls, and, inevitably, someone would come out and tell me to stop. Junior players were—at best—second-class citizens at Bangor."

He began competing in junior events around Ireland and Northern Ireland and had some success. There were other good young players in his age group, and he became friends with most of them. As his game improved, he began spending more and more time practicing, wanting to be better, wanting to win more often.

"When I was little and spending time with my older cousins, I was mad keen for soccer and, to a lesser extent, for rugby," he says. "But once I got bitten by golf, that was it. That was my sport."

He continued to struggle in school—mostly, his mother insists, because he was bored—but was still considered a musical prodigy as a teenager. He had learned to play the piano and clarinet reasonably well, but most of his talent seemed to lie in his singing voice. By then, Mr. Hunter was training him to sing some opera. As would be the case for most of his life, the person who doubted Feherty the most was Feherty.

"There really weren't a lot of singers—operatic or otherwise—coming out of Northern Ireland in those days," he says. "There was a woman named Norma Burrows who'd had some success but that was it. I didn't think there was a lot of call for someone who could butcher 'Danny Boy.'" Feherty figured out that the last thing the world needed was another mediocre tenor.

For the record, everyone from Ireland knows how to sing "Danny Boy." In one scene from *Belfast*, Buddy's mom explains to a friend, "The Irish were born for leaving. All the Irish really need is a phone, a pint of Guinness, and the sheet music to 'Danny Boy.'"

The only exception to that in Feherty's life is the phone: he almost never answers, taking the Fred Couples approach that if you answer, you run the risk of there being someone on the other end. A text will almost always get a response, although it might be five minutes later or five days later.

Like most of his friends, Feherty discovered alcohol when he was very young. "Probably about fourteen," he says now. "I was a pro shop kid, hung out there with the assistant pros and with some of the other kids at the club. I learned to play snooker and cards. I also started to drink. We'd go hang out in the bike sheds and drink: beer, cheap wine, vodka, whatever we could get our hands on.

"Funny thing is my dad had cut back on his drinking by then. So, I figured I could drink for thirty or forty years and someday give it up whenever I wanted to or felt like it. Now, I tell my kids that they are genetically predisposed to it because of me and my dad.

"I developed a huge capacity for alcohol as a teenager. The only time I didn't drink at all was before a golf tournament. Afterward was a different story, but I never drank before I played golf—as a kid or as a pro."

One of the people Feherty became friends with as a youngster was an older man named Jimmy Martin, who did various jobs around the pro shop. "He used to bathe in the sea every morning, regardless of the temperature," Feherty says. "Once, we went and checked the water temperature after he got out. It was 42 degrees. Never bothered him."

Jimmy Martin spent a lot of time searching for lost golf balls in those same waters, and he often gave some of the balls he found to Feherty, which helped encourage him to go out and play on his own, because he knew if he lost a bunch of golf balls, Mr. Martin would be able to replace them for him quickly.

The pro at Bangor Golf Club when David was very young was a man named Ernie Jones. He saw enough in the young Feherty to start giving him some lessons. But it was the pro who succeeded him, David Jones (no relation) who began to push the teenaged Feherty to chase the dream of becoming a good player.

David Jones had been good enough to play on the European Tour, turning pro in the late 1960s before the European Tour even existed. "It was called the Boys Commonwealth Club Tour back then," he remembers. "We played about twenty-five events a year for very little money. The first year it was called the European Tour [1971], I ran eightieth on the money list and made about £900."

Four years later, after he had married and had a child, David Jones took the club pro job at Bangor—more money and, important for the father of an infant, much less travel. That was the summer that Feherty turned seventeen. He had dropped out of school during his junior year because he was bored and didn't enjoy going at all. "I think it was in the middle of a discussion one day in geography class when the teacher was talking about the average rainfall in Western Samoa," he says. "That was the straw that broke the camel's back. I thought, 'what the hell am I doing here?' I'm ready to move on with my life. It wasn't as if I was going to go on to university from there. I never even thought about sitting for the precollege exams. I figured I'd be a disaster anyway."

When David informed his parents he had dropped out of school, they were less than thrilled. "He told us the headmaster had said if he wasn't willing to carry on studying he might as well drop out," his mother says. "There wasn't much to be done at that point."

By then, Feherty had become enamored of golf. He was a good junior player, traveling with friends to junior tournaments around Northern Ireland. "We never had a place to stay," he remembers. "We'd just sleep somewhere on the golf course that looked comfortable and—preferably—dry. Pine straw was always our best bet."

Feherty was already spending more and more time at the golf club, and David Jones took him under his wing, both as a golfer and as a person. "He was always involved in one thing or another around the club," Jones remembers. "He was a moderately talented player at that point, which reminded me a lot of me as a teenager. I was a 7-handicap when I turned pro, but I became a reasonably successful professional.

"I saw that sort of potential in David because he was fearless. He had no quit in him. If he was behind in a match at the turn, he saw the back nine as a place where he could turn things around—and, more often than not, he would turn things around and he'd come back and win the match. I knew he could get better if he had the chance to really work on his game. I had done the same thing as a kid. He had at least as much potential, probably more, than I did."

When he was sixteen, Feherty finished third in the Munster Boys Championship, one of Ireland's most important junior tournaments. It was a US Amateur type of event: thirty-six holes of stroke play with the top sixty-four players qualifying for match play. Feherty lost in the semifinals but won the consolation match to finish third. By then, he was thinking he might have a future in golf. Or at least *wanted* to have a future in golf.

A year later, after dropping out of school, Feherty had to decide whether to pursue a singing career or a golf career. He chose golf. "To this day, I can't tell you why, other than I really wanted to give it a try," he says. "I didn't think I was that good as a singer, and even though I wasn't that good at golf, I *liked* it more. So, I figured if I was going to fail at something it might as well be something I liked a lot and enjoyed. When I told my friends, the ones I had played golf with all my life, that I was going to turn pro they all laughed at me. The notion I could succeed seemed pretty far-fetched to them. Probably to me too."

Billy Feherty was less than thrilled with the notion of his son becoming a golf pro—especially since he was a 5-handicap, meaning he was a solid amateur player but hardly someone ready to make a career as a pro.

Two people convinced him to not get in David's way: David's older sister, Helen, and David Jones.

"His dad came to me and said, 'You have to talk him out of this,'" Jones remembers. "I said to him, 'You've got to give him a chance to find out for himself. If you don't, he'll never completely forgive you.' I really felt that his competitiveness would give him a chance to get good. I'd been where he was as a teenager, and when I started playing full time, I got good pretty fast. I thought it could happen for him too."

For similar reasons, Helen also pushed her parents to let David take a shot at playing golf, although she admits that David enlisted her help.

"He asked me to talk to them," she says, laughing now at the memory. "He thought if I was on his side, it would help."

Vi Feherty was torn. "I wanted him to do something that would make him happy, but I really didn't see any way back then that he could make a good living playing golf," she says. "I still wonder what might have happened if he had stuck with music. But given the way things turned out, I guess he made the right choice."

The final decision was made when Jones convinced an old friend from his playing days, John Farmer, to hire David as an assistant pro at Mid-Hertfordshire Golf Club, which was outside London. Like Jones, Farmer had given up the grind of a low-paying tour to become a club pro.

David's salary was ten pounds a week. The club found him a room to rent for five pounds a week with a club member. The only complication was that David's landlord was gay and found the teen-aged Feherty very attractive. "I spent three months locked in my room every night," he says. "I was terrified. Didn't sleep at all. Plus, I missed Mum."

His decision to leave Mid-Herts—as the club was called—was as much about missing Vi as anything. He returned to Bangor and got a job at nearby Royal Belfast. From there, he moved to Holywood Golf Club, which was less than four miles down Bangor Road from

Royal Belfast. Holywood would become famous later as the club that produced Rory McIlroy, but this was a dozen years before McIlroy was born. David did, however, become friends with McIlroy's parents—Gerry and Rosie. Gerry was the bartender at the club and David spent a good deal of time at the bar.

"Loved them both," he says. "Just the nicest people in the world. It's easy to see why the kid turned out as well as he did. Of course, when the child was born, they must have dropped him on his head. Otherwise, how could he have become so fucking brilliant?"

Contrary to a comment NBC's Dan Hicks made to Feherty during the 2022 British Open, "You've known Rory since he was a kid," Feherty didn't know him as a kid. He does remember seeing him from a distance on a visit to Holywood when McIlroy was about ten.

"He was coming up to the eighteenth green and someone pointed him out to me," he remembers. "They said, 'That's Gerry and Rosie's kid.' He was carrying his bag, and he was walking as if he owned the place. He just had this look. You could see it even then. He just had *it*—whatever *it* is. Without seeing him hit a shot, I thought, 'This kid's going to be a star.' One of the few times in my life I got something right."

After a year at Holywood, David was hired at Bangor Golf Club. The pro there was Fred Daly, who had won the Open Championship in 1947 and had played on four Ryder Cup teams. In those days, being a major champion didn't make you an instant multimillionaire; it meant you had a chance to get a good club pro job when your playing days were over.

Daly, who had grown up in Portrush—which is about sixty miles from Belfast—had the same kind of sense of humor as Feherty, who loved working for him.

"He was in his late sixties when I got there, but he could still play," Feherty says. "Little guy, maybe five-foot-four, but he could still hit the ball. I remember one day he missed a green and found a pot bunker. He hit an excellent shot from there to a couple of feet from the hole. As he walked out of the bunker, he said to me, 'I'm just not very good getting out of bunkers anymore.'

"I said, 'Fred, that was a great shot, what are you talking about?'

"He looked at me and said, 'I'm talking about my *body*. I can get the ball out just fine. It's getting my body out of the bloody things I have trouble with.'"

Sometimes, Feherty would watch Daly give lessons—which Daly didn't do very often because he didn't enjoy it. "More often than not, his way of teaching was to say, 'Copy this,' and then he'd swing the club. Well, if everyone could copy him, they'd all end up as Open champions, right?"

One afternoon, Feherty watched Daly give a lesson to a very good young player named Garth McGimpsey. He and Feherty were the same age, the difference being that Garth was still an amateur and a member at Balmoral while David was Daly's assistant.

"Garth's dad, Hal, was one of *those* fathers," Feherty remembers. "Whenever Garth took a lesson from Fred, he'd come out and watch and stand there taking notes. On this day, Fred stops suddenly and walks over to a grassy area near a corrugated fence that separated our range from a place called King's Hall, where boxing matches were often held.

"Fred takes the club in his right hand and starts swinging it backhand at the grass near the fence. Hal's taking notes the whole time. After a while, Hal walks over and he says, 'Fred, what is that, what is it you're trying to show Garth?' And Fred says, 'Yup, it's true, the crabgrass here is killing the grass on the range.'"

Feherty and Garth McGimpsey got along well, were good friends. Not so their fathers. By then, Billy Feherty had become emotionally invested in his son's golf career, in part because he'd improved, in part because he was his father.

"We used to have a saying, 'daddy-no-caddy,'" David says. "None of us really wanted our dads around when we were playing, and no one wanted them around taking notes during a lesson. When my dad came out to watch me play, I'd get pissed to the point where he'd show up in disguises or he'd dart from tree to tree hoping I wouldn't see him. He and Hal McGimpsey used to argue all the time about who was the better player, Garth or me. It was probably Garth."

By then, Feherty was a much better player than he had been when he first got to Balmoral. He stayed at the club for two life-changing years. The membership of the club was entirely Catholic. The only Protestants on the grounds on a daily basis were Feherty, Daly, and Daly's son, Robin. Every morning, Feherty would leave his parents' house and drive straight up Lisburn Road. "Right into the war zone," he says. "The entire area was an IRA stronghold. There was a peace wall there, about eighty feet high. It's still there to this day."

"Peace walls," as they were euphemistically called, had sprouted throughout Northern Ireland during the Troubles to separate Catholic neighborhoods from Protestant neighborhoods.

"It wasn't as if it was truly dangerous," Feherty says. "You'd occasionally get stopped for an ID check, but that was pretty much it. Still, there wasn't a day that went by that I didn't feel a little bit nervous driving through there."

He made it unscathed each day for two years. And he flourished at Balmoral, growing as a player under Daly and enjoying the membership. "The place was like a fall-down-funny set of a soap opera," he says. "There were so many characters there it was just fun to go to work every day. It was *not* a membership that took itself seriously."

It was impossible not to be aware of the Troubles, even once he had safely negotiated Lisburn Road each day. Balmoral's clubhouse was blown up twice while he was working there. "Once, we were down the street at a club called Dun Murry playing in a little pro-am event," he says. "I remember clearly hearing this popping sound and we knew right away what it was because the sound had become so familiar through the years. The other time, I was out on the golf course somewhere. Most of the time, before a bomb went off almost any place, there was a warning. The clubhouse was destroyed both times, but nobody died. It had been emptied out before the bomb went off."

After two years of working on his game and working with Daly, Feherty had become a much better player. He'd had to lie about his handicap to turn pro, claiming he was a scratch and not a five. Fortunately, in those days, there was no competency test as there is now for anyone wanting to turn pro and get a job as an assistant pro at a golf club. Once upon a time, lying about your handicap to turn pro wasn't uncommon. Ian Poulter, who went on to become a European Ryder Cup star, did the same thing years later.

Being an assistant pro had given Feherty time to work obsessively on his game. The men he worked for had given him guidance, but for the most part, his improvement came about because of hours grinding on the range.

But the turning point came in the winter of 1977 and 1978. A Welsh businessman named Walter Howe put together a group of six young players from the United Kingdom and paid for them to move to Florida—specifically Orlando—to play mini-tours. Feherty was one of the six, given permission by Fred Daly to go since there wasn't much golf played in Northern Ireland during the winter months.

"Howe was hoping, I think, that one of us would pan out and eventually make him a lot of money," Feherty says. "I don't think I was the best player in the group at the time, but I definitely got better while I was over there."

In addition to paying their expenses, Howe set the young players up to take lessons from Phil Ritson, a South African who had become the director of golf at Disney World. Ritson was a decorated and well-known teacher. Years later, in 1997, he founded Orange County National, a few miles down the road from Disney World, just off I-4. It is a public facility with thirty-six holes that are highly regarded enough that it has hosted the PGA Tour's qualifying school finals on several occasions. Ritson had been a very good player before turning to teaching full time and Feherty enjoyed working with him.

Even so, the setup for Feherty and the other five players wasn't perfect. In return for paying expenses, Howe took 50 percent of his players' winnings. "Not a great deal for any of us," Feherty says. "It wasn't as if any of us were making that much, but if we ever did, Howe was going to make a killing. I think that was the idea."

Feherty didn't go to Florida alone. He had dated a girl named Paddy Johnson while in high school, and she traveled with him to the United States. They were engaged for a while, although the relationship faded when Feherty became a full-time, on-the-road golf pro.

In Florida, he got to play a lot of golf. At Bangor, Feherty actually had three jobs: assistant pro, bartender, and paperboy. "I was getting paid fifteen pounds a week at the golf club," he says. "I worked at night at a bar called The Viking. It was a rough place. Lots of fights. The bouncers were kept busy. Wasn't the ideal job for someone who drank as much as I did. But the pay was pretty good."

In Orlando, his only job was to work on his golf game. Working with Ritson helped a great deal; the hours on the range helped and competing week in and week out on the mini-tours helped. All six of Howe's players went to the first stage of PGA Tour Qualifying School that year, played at nearby Greenlefe Golf and Tennis Club. None of them made it to the second stage, and Feherty, in his words, "shot a million." But the experience of playing under that kind of pressure benefited him.

Feherty had actually won a tournament soon after turning pro: the Ladies Tankard Pro-Am, a local event in Belfast in which male pros played with female amateurs. Feherty won the professional event and went home with a check for £5.00, which was worth about $7.50 back then.

Feherty had first played the European Tour qualifying school in 1977 at Foxhills Country Club, which is in Surrey, north of London. Even though he believed he was a much better player than he had been when he turned pro, he was still only nineteen, and he played poorly, failing to come close to making the tour. In addition to his inexperience, the golf course simply didn't suit his left-to-right game.

"If they'd kept Q-school at Foxhills, David might never have made it through," David Jones says with a laugh. "It wasn't in very good shape, and it was very narrow. David's game just wasn't ready for that sort of golf course."

European Tour Q-school was still at Foxhills a year later, and once again, Feherty didn't come close to making it through.

"I just didn't like the golf course," he says. "For one thing, it was in terrible shape. I mean, you could literally see sewage around the course while you were playing. Plus, being honest, I just wasn't good enough yet. Better players could deal with poor conditions. I couldn't."

Feherty vividly remembers some of the anger he felt when people at Balmoral laughed at him for even attempting Q-school again after his failure the first time around. "Most people thought I was crazy," he says. "I remember my uncle Jack laughing and asking if I was actually serious about trying. A lot of people at Balmoral said, 'He's not even as good as Garth McGimpsey. How can he possibly think he's good enough to make it to the tour?' They were probably right, I don't think I was as good a player as Garth at that point. That didn't stop me from giving it another shot."

The two misses at Foxhills were difficult to deal with emotionally. Intellectually, he might have understood that the golf course wasn't suited for his game and his game still had a lot of growing to do. Dealing with it emotionally was another story.

"If I'd been in a position to get a diagnosis back then, they would have told me I was clinically depressed," he says. "Depression is sadness with no hope. That's where I was at that stage of my life. I just didn't understand it."

After his time in Florida, he was a better player when he took his second crack at Foxhills, but still didn't come close to making the cut. That was when the undiagnosed depression kicked in.

"I was in a very dark place, especially after that second time at Foxhills," he says. "I was in that place where I felt sadness with no hope every day. Just getting out of bed in the morning was difficult.

Of course, at that point in my life, I had no idea that I was depressed or bipolar. All of that came later."

He didn't, however, give up. The next fall, he caught a break: Q-school was held at Golf Club Vilamoura in Portugal, the European Tour having finally had enough of Foxhills. This time, Feherty made it through with ease, finishing third. Remarkably, he'd gone from being a 5-handicap in 1975 at the age of seventeen to being a member of the European Tour in 1980 at the age of twenty-two. It was an incredible transformation.

Like the PGA Tour in those days, the European Tour only had sixty fully exempt players. That meant everyone joining the tour out of Q-school had to play in Monday qualifying. In 1980, Feherty only qualified for seven tournaments. A year later, he only got into seven tournaments again.

"It was a tough time," he says. "Every Monday was nerve-racking because if you didn't qualify, you made no money and didn't have a chance to play again for a week. I had some weeks where I just missed and others where I missed by a lot. Either way, it didn't matter. You weren't playing on Thursday."

The only saving grace during that period was the presence of David Jones, who had decided to play the tour part time again after Feherty qualified in Portugal. The two men traveled together in a 1966 Vauxhall Viva with holes in the floorboards that David had bought for sixty pounds after his Q-school success.

"I sold it later to a company that used it for scrap," he says, laughing. "It could have been scrap when I owned it."

Jones's presence was a calming influence on Feherty, who tended to play very well or very poorly. "If he got hot, he could easily shoot 67 because he had plenty of talent," Jones says. "But the next day he might very well go out and shoot 79 if things didn't go well at the start. You could see it was there, that he had the potential to become a very good player. The key was learning to turn those 79s into 72s. Once he started doing that, he took off.

"Golf is a mental game. David always had the swing and he had ability. He just had to learn to consistently believe in that ability. Once he started to do that, he became a very good player."

Feherty always points out the difference between a good player and a great one. "I never believed I could be great," he says. "I always saw myself as a step or two down from the best players. Plus, I always had that self-destructive streak just below the surface. I never really know when it's going to jump up and bite me—on or off the golf course."

CHAPTER THREE

Ryder Cup

THE TROUBLES WOULD CONTINUE IN Northern Ireland until the signing of the Good Friday Agreement in 1998. That didn't completely end them but signaled the beginning of the end. According to historians, 3,507 people were killed during that violent era, and about 107,000 were wounded. Beyond that, the Troubles emotionally damaged countless people, especially children, in Northern Ireland.

"It was impossible not to be affected," Feherty says. "I look back on my childhood and realize there was a lot of fear involved, even though my parents did everything they could to make our lives as normal as possible. But the honest truth is there was nothing normal about it. The numbers you read can't begin to calculate how many people were wounded, emotionally scarred by it all. I didn't have any physical injuries, but there's no doubt I was wounded and so were my sisters by what we lived through as children.

"I was lucky that I found a way out that came naturally, not through being forced to leave. I always came home, I still go home now. But once I made it to the tour, I was traveling nonstop. It just became my life."

A life that would lead him to many places both for good and for bad.

Soon after making it to the tour for the first time, Feherty met Sam Torrance.

Torrance remembers meeting Feherty at a Monday pro-am and being impressed with him from the beginning—as a player and as a person.

"He was younger than me [five years] and not as experienced because I'd been out there a few years by then," Torrance says. "But you could see he was a good player with the potential to become a very good player.

"It was very clear to me from the first time that I played with him. He had a very good golf swing, and he was always fun to play with because he took golf seriously but never took himself seriously. We started playing practice rounds together all the time right away. Every so often, he'd miss a few putts and lose confidence, but the golf swing was always there. He was never as confident as I thought he should be. He never completely understood, in my opinion, just how good he was.

"Even after he started to win tournaments, finish high on the money list—make a Ryder Cup team—he never understood just how good he was. He knew he was good, but he never really believed he could be great. It was as if he didn't think he was worthy of being great."

Torrance was Scottish; Feherty, Irish. They became inseparable. Torrance's father, Bob, was a revered swing teacher, who worked with—among others—major champions Padraig Harrington, Ian Woosnam, Vijay Singh, and Darren Clarke through the years. He also taught Lee Westwood, who never won a major but was briefly ranked number one in the world and played on eleven European Ryder Cup teams. Bob Torrance's favorite pupil was his son, who won forty-four times worldwide, was ranked as high as thirteenth in the world, played on the European Ryder Cup team eight times, and was Europe's (winning) captain in 2002.

"Playing on Ryder Cup teams was thrilling," he says. "But being captain, that was another level. The feeling of responsibility and the feeling of joy when we won. I never had a golf moment that was comparable to that."

Bob Torrance was friends with Ben Hogan—they had met at the 1953 British Open at Carnoustie, the only time Hogan ever played (and won) that championship. He believed in Hogan's teaching principles:

Keeping the left arm tight to the body; improving through practice and drills, not through over-teaching; keeping the golf swing as simple—and as compact—as possible. He didn't believe that one needed a long or wild swing to hit the ball a long way. His swing was living proof of that.

Sam Torrance was the perfect companion for Feherty. The two men were both bitingly funny—though different since one was Irish and one was Scottish. To this day, Feherty is rarely left without an answer to someone, but on occasion Torrance got the last word and still does.

In 1991, when Feherty made the Ryder Cup team, the Europeans flew into the airport in Charleston, South Carolina, on the Concorde. In those days, the visiting team always flew across the Atlantic in the supersonic plane.

When the plane landed, Feherty, sitting in the window seat, was stunned to see hundreds, if not thousands, of people waiting to greet the team. He turned to Torrance, sitting next to him, and said, "I never realized the Ryder Cup was such a big deal over here."

Torrance looked at him and said, "They're here to see the fucking plane, you idiot."

The two men enjoyed playing practical jokes on one another almost nonstop. Feherty's favorite happened at a tournament outside Versailles. The tournament gave out an award—a very expensive watch—to the player who had the low round of the week. Torrance had shot 63 in the second round and, during the prize-giving after the final round, was to be presented with the watch by Isabella Rossellini—daughter of Ingrid Bergman.

"She was considered the most beautiful woman in the world at the time," Torrance says, still laughing at the memory. "Before I went to receive the award, I went into the bar to find David to make our plans for afterward. I could tell when I walked in he was up to something. He knew I was going to receive the award from Rossellini and that I was very excited about it.

"As I started to go, he grabbed a pitcher of water off the bar and threw it right on my crotch, leaving, as you might expect, a massive stain. There was no time to go change or for it to dry off. The pants were gray. I had to walk 40 yards to get to Miss Rossellini with this stain. As she handed me the watch I said to her, 'My best mate just threw water on me.' She cracked up.

"I did too . . . later."

It was almost inevitable that Torrance would eventually convince Feherty that he could become a better player if he went to work with his father. Feherty had played solidly when he first got on tour in 1980, but he became a star after he started working with Bob Torrance.

"It wasn't so much anything he did to change my swing," Feherty says. "If anything, he simplified it for me. Got me to think less—which was always a good thing for me, especially when I was playing golf.

"What he did most was change my attitude. He convinced me that I really could play; that a bad shot, a bad round, even a bad week didn't mean I'd forgotten how to play the game. It just meant I'd hit a bad shot, had a bad round, or had a bad week. If Nicklaus could have an occasional bad week, if Seve could have a bad week, I could have one too. That was always a tough concept for me to grasp, even when I started to play really well."

It took Feherty a couple of years to start playing well on a regular basis, but in 1982, he got into fifteen tournaments and finished fifty-first on the money list. That ended his days as a rabbit, bouncing from tournament to tournament—no more Monday qualifying. After that, he steadily improved, reaching twenty-sixth on the money list in 1983. After slipping to fifty-fourth a year later, he jumped to fifteenth in 1985. A year later, he finally got his first victory, winning the Italian Open in early March.

He was tied going into the final round with Ballesteros, his hero and future BFF. Playing in the last group, Feherty shot 68—to beat Ballesteros by three shots. He still had to win a playoff against Ronan Rafferty, who shot 64 that day to tie Feherty.

He won £23,227—and 77 cents—for the win, which felt like a king's ransom at the time.

"The tournament was played that year on an island called Alberella, that was part of Venice," Feherty says. "There were no cars allowed on the island. We were all staying in apartments near the golf course, and they gave everyone—players and caddies—courtesy *tricycles* to get back and forth each day. It was too funny to see. We looked like a swarm of circus bears heading over there every morning. Maybe I won because I spent the whole week laughing. That and the fact that Seve wasn't really Seve on Sunday."

In addition to the check, Feherty received a handsome trophy. When he had finished his post-round interviews and been given the trophy, he hopped on his tricycle for the ride back to the hotel. "I stuck the trophy into the front basket of the tricycle," he says. "I wish I had a picture of that. I had to ride through a lot of fans who were leaving. I got a few comments from them to say the least."

That was also the week that established Feherty as an accomplished opera singer—at least in the minds of European golf fans. After his victory, he was interviewed on BBC radio. The interviewer was aware of the fact that he had once been an aspiring singer. He asked Feherty if he could perhaps sing something for him.

Feherty instantly burst into song, singing something called "Just One Cornetto." It was *not* from an opera but from a television commercial for an ice cream cone. The commercial featured someone singing the song as if it were part of an opera. Feherty sang it with so much gusto that many—including the interviewer—were convinced that it *was* part of an opera.

"I don't think I sang it all that well," he says. "But I did sing it on key. I could always sing on key."

By the time he won in Italy, Feherty was married. He had traveled often to South Africa as a young player because he had an aunt and uncle who lived in Durban he could stay with and because he could play on the South African Tour during the winter months. During his career he won three times on the Sunshine Tour in South Africa.

Not long after he'd started to play well on the European Tour, he met Caroline DeWit, who told David she had finished third in a South African beauty contest a few years earlier.

"I took her out at first as a favor to a friend," Feherty says, many years later. "My friend said, 'Look, she's beautiful, but she's also bat-shit crazy.' He was right on both counts. She was staggeringly beautiful. And staggeringly bat-shit crazy.'"

Feherty now talks about his first marriage during his stand-up routine and can laugh about it. But there was very little that was funny about the marriage. "It was a nine-year hostage situation" is how he describes it. "I knew early on that I'd made a terrible mistake, but I thought I had to see it through—somehow.

"Then the boys came along, and I was desperate to make it work. In the end, looking back now, there really was no chance. The worst part of it is that the boys caught a lot of the worst of it. I blame myself for allowing that to happen."

Feherty believes now that Caroline saw him as her ticket out of South Africa. He was making decent money by the time they first started dating in 1983, and even though his home was still in Bangor and Northern Ireland wasn't exactly glamorous, he traveled all over Europe to play golf. The couple had a home in Bangor but also kept a home in South Africa because David was still playing on the Sunshine Tour during the European Tour's winter off-season and because Caroline's family was there.

"At its absolute best, the marriage was bad," Feherty says. "My drinking and drug use got a lot worse during the marriage. It's unfair to blame those sorts of problems on anyone but yourself, and I certainly drank long before I met her. But drinking became my way to ease the pain of the marriage and what my life had become at that point. It was my way of not feeling the pain I felt every day. It became my escape from the misery I was feeling."

Feherty was almost the dictionary definition of a functioning alcoholic during that period. He continued not to drink before he played golf, and he continued to improve as a player throughout the eighties.

"I never really saw him as an alcoholic in those days," Torrance says. "He drank after we played and after tournaments, but we all did. It wasn't as if his drinking stood out as being any different from the rest of us."

It was different though, and it got worse as the marriage fell apart. He smoked marijuana and had bouts with more serious drugs—cocaine often and heroin once. And yet, he continued to play good golf. The brush with heroin came in Hong Kong. He finished second that week.

Later in 1986, Feherty won for the second time, winning the Scottish Open at Haggs Castle Golf Club in Glasgow. He remembers the victory: he beat future major champion Ian Baker-Finch and Irish Ryder Cupper Christy O'Connor Jr. in a playoff. He remembers nothing about the next forty-eight hours.

"I woke up two days later to the right of the sixteenth green at Gleneagles," he says. "Gleneagles is about fifty miles from Haggs Castle. I have absolutely no idea how I ended up there. The worst part was that the trophy was gone. To this day, I have no idea how I lost it or when I lost it, and it was never found."

Feherty vaguely remembers partying with members of the band Led Zeppelin on Sunday night. After that, everything is a blank until Peter Grant, the group's manager, poked him with a walking stick two days later to wake him up.

"I *did* still have the check, fortunately. I remember I felt great when I woke up. I must have been asleep for quite a while. The only problem was that I had dew all over me from sleeping in the wet grass."

Feherty continued to play well the next two years. He had finished nineteenth on the money list in 1986, and he dropped to forty-sixth in 1987 and fortieth in 1988—still solid golf but without another victory.

Then, in 1989, he won the BMW Championship, one of Europe's most important events, and finished tenth on the money list. A year later, he didn't win, but he finished second on three occasions and third once. That jumped him to eighth on the money list and into serious contention to make the Ryder Cup team in 1991.

He also captained Ireland's Dunhill Cup team in the fall of 1990. The Dunhill Cup had started in 1985 and was a unique event on the European Tour. It consisted of sixteen three-man teams representing their countries and was played on the Old Course at St. Andrews. Each team match was three singles matches—all stroke play.

Ireland's team that year consisted of Ronan Rafferty, Philip Walton, and Feherty—who, as the highest-ranked player on the team, was the captain. Ireland advanced to the final to play England. The final was six matches—the three players from each team playing the three players on the opposing team twice.

After six matches, the score was tied 3–3. It was a difficult, windy day at St. Andrews. No one had broken 70, and only Rafferty had broken par, twice shooting 71 to win both his matches with Richard Boxall.

With the score tied, the two captains played a four-hole aggregate score playoff. As the R&A does when there is a British Open playoff at St. Andrews, the players played one and two and then crossed from the second green to the seventeenth tee to play seventeen and eighteen. Feherty had a one-shot lead going to seventeen—the infamous Road Hole.

Feherty hit a perfect tee shot and found the fairway, the hole fitting his left-to-right shot perfectly. From there, he had 189 yards to the narrow green into a stiff breeze.

"Anyone with a brain in his head runs the ball up in that situation," Sam Torrance says. "*He* flies it into the wind and hits a perfect cut right at the flag."

"I've never claimed to have a brain in my head," Feherty says. "To this day, I'm not sure how I pulled it off."

He did pull it off though and had an easy two-putt for par. Clark made a double-bogey six on the hole, effectively putting an end to the match.

"That was a big deal," Feherty says. "A lot of the best players were there, and we were all representing our countries, which made it a bigger deal."

Among those who played that year were Greg Norman, Sandy Lyle, Ian Woosnam, and Wayne Grady—all major champions. The US team, which lost to France, consisted of Curtis Strange, Mark Calcavecchia, and Tom Kite—all men who also won major titles.

The day also proved important for Feherty when the Irish national anthem was played during the awards ceremony. There might have been some doubt as to which anthem would be played since Northern Ireland is part of the United Kingdom. But Rafferty and Walton were, as the Irish say, "from the south," so the Irish anthem was played. As he heard the music, a chill went through Feherty.

"I'd honestly never thought about it one way or the other before," he says. "But when they played the anthem, I felt this chill and got choked up, and I thought, "Fuck, what do you know, I'm Irish."

There was no official prize money attached to the Dunhill Cup, but Feherty's play under pressure in a team event wasn't likely to go unnoticed by new European Ryder Cup captain Bernard Gallacher—who had taken Tony Jacklin's place after Europe had lost (barely) under Jacklin in 1983 and then won under him in 1985 and 1987 and retained the Cup in 1989. After that, he decided it was time for someone else to deal with the pressures that came with the captaincy. That someone turned out to be Gallacher.

If there had been any doubts about whether Feherty would be on the 1991 team, they went away when he won in Cannes in early April, beating Australian Craig Parry by three strokes. Although the team wasn't formally named until after the Open Championship in July—won that year at Royal Birkdale by a non–Ryder Cupper Australian, Ian Baker-Finch—Feherty was a lock to qualify after the win in Cannes.

By then, he was a father. Shey had been born in 1988, but the marriage hadn't gotten any better. A second son, Rory, would come along in 1992, but Feherty's hopes that the arrival of children might save the marriage were dashed pretty quickly.

"Caroline was always a very needy person," he says, "and back then, between my career and my drinking, I wasn't very much of a dad. It was a bad situation. Until it got worse."

Feherty was thrilled to make the Ryder Cup team, even though he knew Europe would be a heavy underdog playing on US soil with the Americans desperate for their first win since 1983. The matches were going to be played on Kiawah Island's newly opened Ocean Course. Kiawah Island is on the South Carolina coast, and designers

Pete and Alice Dye wanted it to play as close to the ocean as possible on as many holes as possible. They succeeded, but when the wind blew in from the water, the golf course became almost unplayable, even for the best golfers in the world.

On the day of the singles matches, with twenty-two of the world's best players on the golf course, no one was under par. Two players, Steve Pate and David Gilford, didn't play that day because Pate was injured, and their match was declared a draw without either man hitting a shot.

Once, the Ryder Cup had been little more than a hit-and-giggle event played every two years and dominated by the United States. After a ten-year break from 1937 to 1947 brought about by World War II, the Americans had gone 14–1–1 against Great Britain and Ireland over the ensuing thirty years—losing in 1957 and tying the matches 14–14 in 1969, meaning they retained the Cup.

It was Jack Nicklaus who changed the Ryder Cup forever in 1977. That year, the United States won 12.5–7.5, the format having been changed so that only 20 points would be contested, the thinking being that fewer matches would mean the depth of the American team would be less of a factor.

It didn't matter. In fact, Tom Weiskopf, who was one of the best players in the world at that point and had played for the United States in both 1973 and 1975, decided to pass on playing in the matches.

When Nicklaus called to ask him why he wasn't going to play, Weiskopf said, "You guys don't need me. I'm going hunting."

He was right. They didn't need him. "I realized that year that even though the Ryder Cup was special, playing the matches wasn't special anymore," Nicklaus says. "I also knew there were some very good young players coming from the continent who weren't from

Great Britain or Ireland, most notably Seve. The thought crossed my mind that if we included all of Europe, the matches might be more competitive."

Seve Ballesteros was only twenty at the time but had already tied for second place (with Nicklaus) at the Open Championship a year earlier at nineteen. Three years later, at twenty-two—the same age Nicklaus was when he won his first major—he won the first of his three British Open titles.

Nicklaus's idea to include all of Europe in the matches was quickly accepted by the Ryder Cup committees on both sides of the Atlantic. "I did it because I didn't want the Ryder Cup to die," he says. "We were winning so easily that it had become a blip on the golf calendar. I thought it deserved better than that.

"It should have been a great event, one of *the* events in golf, but at that point, it wasn't. I wanted it to be competitive so it would matter." He laughs. "Little did I know what I had wrought. It's caused a lot of anguish over here [in the United States], but I'm still glad I did it."

The Europeans were open to Nicklaus's idea because they, too, realized the event had become sadly one-sided. "It wasn't that hard to convince us at all," says Ken Schofield, who was executive director of the European Tour at the time. "We were sick and tired of losing—and losing badly. I think Jack recognized that if the event didn't change, it would die, and that would have been a shame for golf."

The new format, United States versus Europe, made its debut in 1979. The Americans won with ease that year and again in 1981. But things began to change in 1983 when the United States—captained by Nicklaus—barely hung on for a 14.5–13.5 victory at PGA National in Palm Beach, Florida. There were three players from the European continent on that team: Ballesteros; Bernhard Langer, a German; and Jose-Maria Canizares, like Ballesteros, a Spaniard.

Two years later, playing at the Belfry in the English Midlands, Europe won for the first time since 1957, easing to a 16.5–11.5 victory. There were four Spaniards on that team along with one German—Langer. The clinching putt was rolled in by a Scotsman named Sam Torrance.

Two years after that, with Nicklaus again the American captain, the matches were played at Muirfield Village in Ohio, the course he had created to host his annual tournament, the Memorial. Led by Ballesteros and another Spaniard, a twenty-one-year-old Ryder Cup rookie named Jose-Maria Olazabal, the Europeans stunned the Americans, 15–13. In one of the more famous scenes in golf history, the Europeans danced on "Jack's green"—the eighteenth at Muirfield Village—after the trophy was presented.

Nicklaus's goal had been accomplished—even if it was painful for him. "Actually, I'm glad I was the captain when they beat us in the US," he says. "It might have destroyed someone else. I could deal with it."

The Ryder Cup was no longer a blip on the golf calendar after that. In 1989, the matches returned to the Belfry, and it appeared the Americans were going to win it back. But four (of twelve) Americans found water on the eighteenth hole on Sunday with singles matches on the line, and Europe was able to rally back to tie, 14–14. That meant the trophy stayed in Europe for two more years.

It also brought about what became known as the War by the Shore in 1991. The name came from the fact that several American players decided to show up in camouflage gear when they arrived, clearly losing sight of the fact that there's a huge difference between actual war and a golf match—no matter how badly you might want to win.

There was a good deal of animosity between the two teams even before the matches started. It began when Steve Pate was injured in a car accident en route to one of the prematch dinners that players were required (in those days) to attend. Pate bruised his ribs in the accident and was taken to the hospital, largely as a precaution. Even so, US captain Dave Stockton had the option to replace him since the matches had not yet started.

Feherty had been involved—indirectly—in Pate's accident. One of the traditions of the Ryder Cup is that players bring their wives or, occasionally, girlfriends to the matches. The wives are considered a major part of the week's activities and, in fact, are introduced during the opening ceremonies.

In 1993, during the opening ceremony at the Belfry, the American wives marched out, two by two, wearing matching outfits selected for them by Linda Watson, then-wife of US captain Tom Watson. It appeared that they were all five-foot, ten-inch blondes, except for Melissa Lehman, a five-foot, ten-inch brunette.

As they marched in, Lewine Mair, the great British golf writer, looked at them and said, "My God, they've all married the same woman."

Caroline Feherty wasn't five-ten, but she was a beautiful blonde who had insisted on being part of the Ryder Cup. David and Caroline were en route to the Wednesday-night gala dinner. A police escort had been assigned to allow the cars to go through red lights without stopping.

"I can't remember exactly what happened, but one of us asked the driver a question," Feherty says. "He turned around to answer the question, and as he did, we came up to a red light that hadn't been cleared. We got halfway into the intersection, and the driver realized what he'd done and slammed on the brake. The two cars behind us couldn't stop in time and rear-ended us and each other. We weren't hurt. The people in the second car weren't hurt, but Pate got hurt.

"We actually kept going, once the driver realized no one was hurt and the car—apparently—wasn't damaged that badly. It wasn't until breakfast the next morning that I found out Steve had been hurt."

It wasn't until months later that Feherty had a chance to tell Pate what had happened. "I don't even remember exactly where we were," he said. "We might have been at Muirfield [site of the 1992 British Open], but I do remember when I told him what had happened, he just looked at me and said, 'You're shitting me.' I told him that, unfortunately, I wasn't in the least."

Stockton opted to keep Pate on the team, but he sat out both sessions on Friday and the morning session on Saturday. He then played on Saturday afternoon, partnering with Corey Pavin in a very competitive 2-and-1 loss to Colin Montgomerie and Langer—one of Europe's strongest teams.

Pate was scheduled to play David Gilford the next day in the singles. The matches were tied 8–8 after two days. On Sunday morning, Stockton informed European captain Bernard Gallacher that Pate's ribs were too sore after Saturday's match for him to play on Sunday. By rule, the Gilford-Pate match was declared a draw, giving each team a half point.

There had been bad blood between the teams before that: Paul Azinger and Ballesteros had gotten into a heated argument over the ball that Azinger and Chip Beck were using on Friday morning, and Ballesteros and Raymond Floyd got into a shouting match on Saturday when Floyd was convinced that Ballesteros's persistent cough was another form of gamesmanship.

On Sunday, many in the European media were convinced that Stockton was trying to guarantee—or steal—a half point by declaring Pate unable to play.

The notion of golf as a "gentleman's game" was long gone by the time singles play began on Sunday.

"I guess we heard Steve wasn't going to play at breakfast on Sunday," Feherty says. "The singles always start later because there's only one session (all twelve singles matches) as opposed to two. I don't think any of us necessarily thought Stockton was trying to pull a fast one. I certainly didn't—especially given my role in what had happened. I do know it came up in the media. The British media, particularly the tabloids, tend to get emotional about the Ryder Cup."

Feherty had played with Torrance on both Friday and Saturday. On Friday afternoon, they halved their fourball (best ball) match with Mark O'Meara and Lanny Wadkins, with Feherty making a ten-foot birdie putt on the eighteenth green to secure the half point. "He won the half point almost single-handedly," Torrance remembers. "First time you play in the Ryder Cup, it can be so overwhelming. It's one of those things that's a little like parenting: it can't be explained to you. You have to experience it to understand it. David handled it unbelievably well. He was brilliant."

"Never been so nervous in my life, before or since," Feherty says. "I was very happy to get the ball airborne on the first tee. After that, Sam more or less talked me through eighteen holes. If I'd played with anybody but him, I might never have finished a hole."

The next morning, Gallacher put Torrance and Feherty out in foursomes (alternate shot) and they lost on the sixteenth hole to Wadkins and Hale Irwin—both major champions. All three Americans Feherty and Torrance faced during those first two days were—or would be in O'Meara's case—major champions. As has often been the case in Ryder Cups dating to 1985, the less decorated Europeans more than held their own.

That was certainly the case on Sunday. The singles began with four-time major champion Nick Faldo facing four-time major champion Raymond Floyd—a match that Faldo won, 2-up, on the eighteenth hole.

Gallacher then sent Feherty out to play Payne Stewart, who had won the second of his three majors titles—the US Open—three months earlier, in June. Stewart was ranked sixth in the world; Feherty, forty-fourth.

Feherty won, 2 and 1.

"In a very real sense, I was lucky to draw Payne," Feherty says. "Not because he wasn't a great player—he was—but because we were friends. I had spent a good deal of time with him when he played in Europe. He was good friends with (photographer) Lawrence Levy, and I was also friends with Lawrence. The three of us hung out together quite a bit. Payne had the kind of evil sense of humor I really enjoyed.

"So, even though I knew the match would be difficult, I was comfortable standing on the first tee because he was a friend. I think that's why I played so well."

Still, the day was anything but easy.

By the time the players turned for the back nine, there was complete chaos all over the property. The wind had come up, making the golf course almost impossible to play. Keeping balls from moving on the greens was a major challenge.

Additionally, security had lost control of the crowds. The American fans had been loud and often vulgar all weekend, but with the matches still in doubt and the possibility of Europe retaining the Cup yet again becoming quite real, they got worse. The marshals were quite vigilant about keeping the American players protected as they walked from greens to tees. It wasn't quite as true of the Europeans.

"The fans were all over the place," Feherty remembers. "The security people and the marshals were trying, but they'd lost control. It was as if the ropes had disappeared completely. Just getting from one green to the next tee was a challenge."

Feherty played superbly on the first few holes of the back nine, building a 4-up lead through fourteen holes. Then, it seemed to dawn on him what he was doing, and he butchered the next two holes, including a tee shot at the sixteenth that landed in the Atlantic Ocean about halfway to Ireland. That meant the margin was down to 2-up through sixteen, and Feherty was in a seriously bad mood as he attempted to walk to the seventeenth tee.

He was again fortunate at that moment that his opponent was Stewart. As great a player as he was, Stewart was also someone who understood that golf was golf—not war. And he understood that the Ryder Cup was supposed to be a competition played in the spirit of the game.

The most famous gesture of Ryder Cup sportsmanship took place in 1969, when Jack Nicklaus conceded a two-foot putt on the eighteenth green at Royal Birkdale, giving Tony Jacklin a halve in their final singles matches and leaving the matches tied, 16–16. Knowing the United States would retain the Cup with a tie, Nicklaus, after making a five-footer of his own for par, picked up Jacklin's mark.

Jacklin later said that as the two men walked off arm in arm, Nicklaus said to him, "I know you would have made that putt, but I wasn't going to give you a chance to miss it."

Even though US captain Sam Snead criticized Nicklaus for the gesture: "We came over here to win, not to be good ol' boys," he told

Sports Illustrated that day, Nicklaus's act has since been hailed as the greatest act of Ryder Cup sportsmanship. Years later, he and Jacklin designed a golf course together in Florida. They called it The Concession.

Fast-forward past Feherty's 1991 match with Stewart to 1999— two years after Feherty had retired—when Stewart actually performed another act of sportsmanship comparable to Nicklaus's but which has gone largely unnoticed through the years. He was paired in the final singles match against Colin Montgomerie in that year's matches at the Country Club in Brookline. That turned out to be the Sunday when the United States rallied from a 10–6 deficit on the final day to win. Montgomerie, who was a rookie on that 1991 team at Kiawah, had become Europe's best Ryder Cup player, and it appeared for a long time that afternoon that the matches would be decided by the outcome of the final match.

As with Kiawah, the American crowd had gotten ugly. Europe had won the Cup in both 1995 and 1997, and the possibility of another loss seemed to be reason enough for many American fans to act like idiots.

Montgomerie was the fans' number one target, in part because he was Europe's best player, in part because of Feherty.

Feherty loves nicknames. Rory McIlroy has two: one is "Scunger," an Irish word for someone who isn't any good at golf. The other is "Eggbert," in honor of Feherty's son Rory.

"When he was born, they had to do what's called a 'ventouse delivery,' where they take a plunger and put it on top of the baby's head in order to get him out of the mother's body," he explains. "Because of that, his head looked like it was shaped like an egg after he was born, so I started calling him Eggbert. Just made sense to me to call Rory [McIlroy] Eggbert too."

And Scunger? "Obviously a bit of irony there."

During his early days working for CBS, Feherty had labeled Montgomerie "Mrs. Doubtfire." Torrance believes the first person to use the term was Englishman Mark Roe, a longtime European Tour player. There's no doubt, though, that it was Feherty who made the nickname famous because Montgomerie *does* look like Robin Williams's character from the 1993 movie. Beyond that, Montgomerie almost never wears a cap and that makes his florid features and often pouty expressions easy for people to see. He also has a temper.

In the right mood, Montgomerie is a delight: he's bright and can be very funny. In the wrong mood, duck—something Feherty found out quite literally during that 1999 Ryder Cup in Boston.

Torrance was one of Mark James's vice-captains for Europe that year, and he asked Feherty to come along to help him out with various logistical issues—like making sure all those who needed carts to get around the chockablock golf course had them.

One night, the Europeans were having dinner in their team room. A buffet had been set up for everyone. As she was going through the buffet, Eimer Montgomerie, the golfer's wife, began screaming at Feherty about the way the American crowds were treating her husband—not only during the Ryder Cup but wherever and whenever he played in the United States.

"It's your fault!" she ranted at Feherty. "It's all your fault! This is all happening because of you!"

Montgomerie was directly behind his wife, loading up what Feherty would later call "the largest Caesar salad I'd ever seen in my life."

As his wife yelled at Feherty, Montgomerie said nothing. Finally, he took the loaded-up plate, wound up, and, with a guttural yell, threw the entire plate and all that was on it directly at Feherty. "I was so shocked I never moved," Feherty says. "One minute, Eimer was yelling at me, the next minute Colin was leaning back—without having said a word—and throwing the entire plate at me."

The plate never reached Feherty. As it flew through the air, a waiter, completely unaware of what was going on, walked in the direction of the buffet table, carrying additional food. At the exact right—or wrong—moment, he walked right in between Feherty and Montgomerie and the salad splattered all over him.

"It was quite a sight," Feherty says. "He never said anything, just knelt down and started picking up the mess. Colin and Eimer walked away without another word. I never found out if Colin got anything to eat that night. I suspect he did."

By Sunday afternoon of that week, the *nicest* thing most people in the crowd following Montgomerie and Stewart were calling Montgomerie was Mrs. Doubtfire. (I was walking with the match and saw and heard it all.) Montgomerie's father, also walking with the two players, simply left the golf course, unable to bear hearing the words directed at his son. On a couple of occasions, Stewart had fans taken out because they had gone *way* past the line of civil behavior.

The most oft-used phrase directed at Montgomerie that day rhymes with "fat runt." Stewart did everything in his power to protect Montgomerie while also trying to win the match, but there was only so much he could do.

The United States ended up winning the Cup when Justin Leonard made a forty-five-foot putt on the seventeenth green to clinch at least a halve against Jose-Maria Olazabal, giving the United States 14.5 points.

All Ryder Cup matches are played out, even after the outcome has been decided, and Stewart and Montgomerie arrived on the eighteenth green with their match even. Montgomerie hit the green in two and had a twenty-five-foot birdie putt to win the match because Stewart had missed the green and had about a six-foot putt for par.

As Montgomerie started to line up his putt, Stewart walked in his direction and pointed at the golf ball. "Pick it up," he said. "It's good."

He was conceding the hole and—thus—the match to Montgomerie. As Stewart walked toward him, Montgomerie, understanding what he was doing, clapped for him before the two men warmly shook hands.

"We'd won the Cup back, that was all I cared about," Stewart said later. "I really didn't care about my individual record. After what Colin had been through that day, no way was I making him putt that."

Tragically, that act of grace turned out to be Stewart's last on the international stage. He was killed four weeks later in a private plane crash.

In 1999, Stewart played the Ryder Cup three months after winning the US Open. The same was true in 1991. He had beaten Scott Simpson in a playoff at Hazeltine in June for his second major title. He had won the 1989 PGA Championship and, at thirty-four, was in the prime of his career.

But on that chaotic Sunday, Feherty was the better player.

"He just beat me," Stewart said years later. "He did a great job controlling his ball in the wind. I wasn't bad, but he was better, especially on seventeen. He hit a truly great shot."

The chaos on the golf course peaked as the players left the sixteenth green, with Feherty's lead down to 2-up. Fans were inside the ropes and running amok. Not surprisingly, security and the marshals managed to get Stewart safely to the seventeenth tee. The same wasn't true for Feherty.

Even though he was wearing an outfit that clearly identified him as a European player and his caddie, Rodney Wooler, was dressed in the European team's caddie outfit and carrying golf clubs, or maybe *because* Feherty was wearing an outfit that identified him as a European player, he literally had to fight his way through the crowds to get near the tee. But when he attempted to walk onto the tee, a female marshal pushed him back and said, "You can't come up here."

"What I remember about that moment was that she was considerably bigger than me," he says. "What I also remember was my mood was such that if she hadn't gotten out of my way, something ugly might have happened—to me."

That was the moment when Stewart, goofy midwestern grin firmly in place, stepped forward and took Feherty's arm. "Ma'am, I understand exactly how you feel about this asshole," he said to the marshal. "But, unfortunately, I need him up here with me."

Feherty still laughs when he tells the story. "Thank God I was playing Payne," he says. "Someone else might not have reacted so coolly. I certainly wasn't about to act coolly until he intervened. I have no idea what would have happened next if Payne hadn't taken control. If there was ever someone who *got* the Ryder Cup and what it was *supposed* to be about, it was Payne."

When he finally got on the tee, Feherty hit the best shot of his life: a 1-iron into the swirling winds aimed at a water-guarded green 243 yards away. "The 4-iron on the Road Hole at St. Andrews in the Dunhill Cup was really good," he says. "But given what was at stake and the way the golf course was playing, the 1-iron was better. Still don't know how I pulled it off."

It was Lee Trevino, Feherty's hero, who once said that the best thing to do in a lightning storm was hold a 1-iron over your head, "because even God can't hit a 1-iron." That day, Feherty hit a godlike 1-iron. Today, no one on tour plays a 1-iron; they all play hybrid woods instead.

Feherty remembers seeing the ball land on the distant green and turning to see Bernard Gallacher, his captain, running off the tee with his arms in the air, celebrating.

"I also remember [former European captain] Tony Jacklin at that moment," he says, laughing. "He was standing with his back to the tee. He couldn't bear to watch."

Having pulled off the miraculous 1-iron, Feherty and Stewart both made par 3s, allowing Feherty to close out the match. At that moment, Europe led 10–8. Soon after, Montgomerie, playing in the third match, rallied from 4-down against Mark Calcavecchia for a half and it looked as if Europe was going to win again. Montgomerie—a Ryder Cup rookie that year who would go on to be one of *the* great Ryder Cup players—finished the match by going double bogey–par–double bogey–par and won all four holes.

"It shows you not just that the golf course was brutally difficult," he said years later, "but what Ryder Cup pressure can do to players."

Calcavecchia was so upset after the match ended, he had to be dragged off the nearby beach by his teammates to watch the rest of the matches. After the United States won, his fellow Americans told him repeatedly that his half point had been critical. Even so, he admitted that he was haunted for years by those last four holes.

Feherty had no such issues. Even playing in a wicked left-to-right wind that could have made the ball fly well right of the green, he beat Stewart, the crowd, and the marshals. That his team lost was disappointing, but the memory of being part of that team still makes him smile.

"Seve [who had gone 3–1–1 for the week] was absolutely gutted that we'd lost," he says. "When he was telling us every night that we were going to win, he absolutely believed it. So did we. We really shouldn't have had a chance to win or even to tie. They were playing at home, they *had* to win, and yet, we were about two inches from taking the Cup back to Europe on the Concorde."

Nineteen years later, in 2010, Feherty became an American citizen and says now he pulls unabashedly for the Americans in the Ryder Cup.

"I'm not sure I ever wanted to win anything more in my life," he says of his weekend as a European Ryder Cupper. "But that was several lifetimes ago."

He smiles. "There are a lot of things in my past I really don't remember that well. But there's nothing about that week that I've forgotten. Losing sucked. But the entire experience was greater than anything I've ever experienced in golf."

As Sam Torrance explains, playing in the Ryder Cup can't be explained, it has to be experienced. Brandt Snedeker, who played on two Ryder Cup teams for the United States, may have summed up the nerves all players feel when he described how he felt on the first tee at Medinah in 2012—his first Ryder Cup.

"Jim Furyk was my partner," he says. "He'd only played in about one hundred of them at that point. [Actually it was Furyk's eighth Ryder Cup.] He gets up on the first tee and hits a snap hook to God knows where. We're playing alternate shot, meaning I'm going to have to go over there and figure out how to hit some kind of shot.

"I should have been thinking, 'What the hell kind of second shot did he just leave me?' Instead, I was thinking, 'Oh thank goodness. If nerves can get to Jim Furyk in the Ryder Cup, then I guess it's OK that my legs are shaking so bad I can barely walk.'"

Feherty came through that weekend, shaking legs and all. It was, to say the least, a memorable experience. As it is for all who take part.

CHAPTER FOUR

Anita

EVEN THOUGH HIS NEW BEST friend Seve Ballesteros thought his name was Doug and even though Europe lost the so-called War by the Shore, David Feherty's golf career was riding high coming out of the 1991 Ryder Cup.

A few weeks prior to the Ryder Cup, he had qualified to play in his first Masters by finishing T-6 in the PGA Championship. In those days, the top eight PGA finishers qualified to play the next year at Augusta, meaning Feherty had a spot in the tournament in April 1992. That PGA, played at Bellerive, outside St. Louis, marked the first time he had played a major in the United States.

He played reasonably well at Augusta, making the cut and finishing tied for fiftieth place. But he didn't feel especially comfortable playing the golf course.

"The whole thing was intimidating," he says. "It felt surreal, even playing practice rounds. The golf course was so pristine, I honestly felt as if the blades of grass they cut were taken to the maintenance shed and put in little tiny hospital beds so they would recover overnight.

"The greens were *so* fast. They would never talk about how fast the greens were—of course they never talked about much. Everything there is a secret."

He smiles. "But I used to spy on them in the mornings when I was in the tower at fifteen when they went out to measure the greens before anyone got to fifteen. They would be out there with the stimp-meter, and I would watch them. The greens were always at least fifteen early in the day. Of course, that wasn't something you talked about on the air."

The obsessively secretive Augusta membership never announces green speeds, but players will tell you they believe some of the greens, especially when they are dried out late on a sunny day, can run as fast as fifteen or sixteen on the stimp-meter, the device that measures green speeds. The stimp-meter is nothing more than a stick that a ball is rolled down and measures how far the ball will roll on the flat portion of a green.

Generally speaking, twelve to thirteen (feet) is considered fast and fourteen is considered very fast. Anything over that is borderline unfair—or perhaps completely unfair.

"I didn't dislike the place when I first played it, I just didn't feel comfortable. The feeling never completely went away. It wasn't as if the people [members] weren't nice, just the opposite, in fact. I just could never shake the fact that it was a place where I didn't belong. Maybe I was subconsciously influenced by the fact that [Lee] Trevino never really felt comfortable there."

By the time Feherty played in the 1991 PGA, he had played in the Open Championship seven times—tying for sixth place in 1989 and contending at St. Andrews in 1990 until a four-putt on the twelfth green on Sunday knocked him backward.

"I was god-awful the rest of the day," he says. "I went from somewhere in the top ten to nowhere in sight [T-68]."

His trip to Crooked Stick in Indianapolis for that PGA was the first time he'd played a major in the United States. In fact, he had only played twice in the United States prior to 1991—qualifying for the 1988 World Series of Golf in Akron and playing the week before in the International as a warm-up. That was it. He wasn't stunned when John Daly came out of nowhere to win the '91 PGA because he'd played with Daly in South Africa. "The golf course where we played was full of doglegs," he says. "I'm not even sure John noticed them. He just hit all his tee shots right over the doglegs. He was blindingly long."

Going into the Ryder Cup, Feherty was ranked forty-fourth in the world. By the following spring, he was ranked thirty-third. Nowadays, when Feherty talks about his golf career, one might get the impression that he played the "B" flight in the Bangor Golf Club championships when he was at his best.

"He made himself into a good player, a very good player," says David Jones, his mentor at Bangor when he was a teenager and in his early days as a pro. "What people didn't really understand was his work ethic. About the only time he stopped hitting balls on the range was when he went out to play. He was constantly searching to make himself a better player."

By the time he reached his peak ranking in 1992, Feherty was using golf and alcohol to escape from the "hostage situation" that he felt his marriage had become. By then, there were two young boys at home, but that didn't make his home life any happier. There were wonderful moments with Shey and Rory, but they were frequently overwhelmed by Feherty's belief that the marriage wasn't going to survive.

"You have to understand, I took the approach that I was in it for the long haul," he says. "I was willing to do almost anything to make it work, to make it better, to try to make her happy. I failed miserably.

"I drank before I got married, but it got much worse afterward," he says. "And I added cocaine to the repertoire. When we were in South Africa, it was easy to get cocaine, much too easy."

Most who know Feherty will tell you that the failure of the marriage was a team effort: Caroline was never happy, and David buried his sorrows in a bottle. Or, more accurately, many bottles—and occasionally marijuana or cocaine.

"Funny thing is, I always thought I could control it," he says. "That's the lie alcoholics tell themselves: I can stop whenever I want. But you don't stop. I didn't stop; I just drank more. I thought, 'When I really need to stop, I'll stop.' But that was never the case."

For a long time though, neither his marriage nor his drinking affected his golf. He played fewer tournaments in Europe in 1992 than in the past because he played several events in the United States since he had qualified to play in the Masters, the US Open, and the PGA. He won again in the fall of 1992 in Madrid and still finished forty-sixth on the European money list in spite of his lighter schedule. A year later, even though he didn't win, he was twenty-second on the money list.

Then he came home the last week in August 1993 after playing in the German Open and found the three-word note from Caroline on the kitchen table. He didn't know it at the time, but the note was the beginning of the end of his golf career.

It wasn't as if his game went directly south at that moment. But his life did—even as he moved west, to Dallas, where Caroline and the boys had gone.

Feherty has nothing nice to say about his ex-wife. He talks about her in his *Feherty Off Tour* stand-up, and it is hysterically funny but tinged with a good deal of sadness.

Feherty had played in twenty European Tour events in 1993 prior to "The Note" and was twenty-second on the money list. He had just turned thirty-five and was in golf's sweet spot: he had plenty of playing experience and had enjoyed a good deal of success but was still young enough to hit the ball plenty long off the tee and had the stamina to finish strong on Sundays. Just as important, regardless of his off-course issues, he was in a good place mentally.

"He was always a good player under pressure," Torrance says. "The Ryder Cup is the best example, but the year before that, in the Dunhill Cup [played at St. Andrews], he hit that shot on the Road Hole [the seventeenth] with the [team] title on the line that was as good as any I've ever seen hit. No one tries to fly an iron onto that green; it's too dangerous. You run it up and hope. [Jack] Nicklaus always ran it up. Everyone did. David took a 4-iron and carved it into the wind and landed it twenty feet from the hole. Ireland won because of *that* shot."

The shot came on the third playoff hole of Feherty's match with England's Howard Clark. Ireland and England had reached the final—each match was eighteen holes of medal play. It was one of those windy days at St. Andrews when the Old Course becomes extremely difficult. When Feherty and Clark finished their match tied, the team match was also tied. So, rather than give each player a half point, the two men played off. Feherty won the match—and, thus, the team title.

Feherty rarely agrees with compliments people pay him—except when they say he's funny, because there's no avoiding that—but agrees that he enjoyed playing under the gun most of the time.

"That was the second-best shot I ever hit in my life [behind only the 1-iron he hit in the Ryder Cup singles a year later at Kiawah]," he says when Torrance's description of the Road Hole 4-iron comes up. "In those days, I did have a lot of confidence under pressure most of the time. Maybe it was because I never saw myself as a great player, so I didn't feel pressure to prove to anyone that I was great. I knew I *wasn't* great. I was good, but never felt I was in that top group of players. So, most of the time when I needed to pull off a shot, I figured, 'What the heck, if you don't pull it off, who's going to even notice?'

"I won the Irish Open [which wasn't a European Tour event] in 1980 and 1982. I should have won three in a row, but in '81 I hit my tee shot on eighteen on Sunday into the water when I was tied for the lead. Flat-out choke, no other way to explain it. That's the only time I can remember hitting a shot that mattered that was an absolute choke.

"What happened at Turnberry the last day in '94 [Open Championship] was different. My hands didn't shake, I didn't feel any more nervous than usual. In fact, I remember enjoying playing both days of the weekend with Fuzzy [Zoeller]. But when I look back on the putts I missed around the turn, I honestly think I just didn't think myself worthy of being an Open champion," Feherty says, confirming Sam Torrance's speculation. "My life was a mess at that point. I didn't think I'd do well dealing with all that comes with being an Open champion. Being a good player is one thing. Being a major champion is another. I think, subconsciously, I didn't want to deal with what would have come with being an Open champion. I wanted to win; I just don't think I wanted what would have come if I'd won."

It wasn't as if he went sky-high the last day at Turnberry. He shot an even-par 70 and finished T-4. Nick Price eagled the seventeenth hole—on a fifty-foot putt—shot 66, and won the championship.

By then, Feherty was a full-fledged member of the PGA Tour. Reluctantly, he had followed Caroline—or, more accurately, he'd followed the boys—to Texas. If he wanted to be near his sons, he had no choice but to get a place in Dallas. That meant he had to play his golf in the United States and that meant going to PGA Tour Qualifying School.

His status in Europe—five-time winner; Ryder Cupper; twenty-second on the 1993 money list—was worth the price of a cup of coffee as far as those running the PGA Tour were concerned. Actually, it didn't even get him a cup of coffee, and this was before coffee cost four dollars a cup.

That's why he had to go to Q-school and play through all three stages. Fortunately, his game was sharp, and he breezed, securing full status on tour in 1994.

He played in twenty-two PGA Tour events that year and finished 100th on the money list, earning $178,501, meaning he retained his playing privileges for 1995 since the top 125 finishers remained fully exempt. His best finish in the United States came the week after his T-4 at Turnberry when he finished second to Kenny Perry in the New England Golf Classic, missing a playoff by one shot.

Those two performances jumped him from 155th on the money list to 80th on the money list. He played sparingly that fall, knowing his spot on the tour was secure for 1995. That gave him the chance to be at home with his kids. He and Caroline were finally getting a divorce, and David was living in a two-bedroom apartment, often with two small boys.

"Whenever I was home, I had them," he says, "which was a good thing, except living in a two-bedroom apartment with two small boys wasn't easy under the best of circumstances, and there was nothing best about my life at that point."

He was still drinking and still using drugs—"a full-blown addict" is how he describes himself at that time. He was also beginning to deal with serious depression issues that he didn't fully understand, and he was running "like Forest Gump," he jokes, to the point where he weighed less than 150 pounds. That was why Anita Schneider wondered if he was HIV positive on their first date.

Anita Fortenberry had grown up in the tiny community of Cato, which was located in Rankin County, Mississippi, on a soybean and cotton farm. She was the youngest of three children, and her parents divorced when she was five, leaving her to be raised by an aunt and uncle.

At sixteen, having graduated from high school early, she moved to Jackson and enrolled in business school. Several jobs later, she was hired as one of the first female car saleswomen in Mississippi. "I sold a lot of cars," she says, laughing. "Everyone wanted to say they'd bought their car from the woman salesperson."

Anita moved to Houston when she was offered the chance to get into a management program. It was there that she met Fred Schneider, who was the son of the man who owned the dealership where she was working.

"He was actually building a ranch when I started working there," she says. "When he came back to work, he asked me to lunch, and it went from there."

They got married and had two sons—Fred and Karl—and Anita stopped working, in part because it wasn't easy being married to the son of the dealership's owner, in part because she had two little boys to raise.

When the marriage ended in divorce, she started a home design business that she was able to run from home—allowing her to work and take care of her boys. Then, in 1995, she and her sons moved to Dallas. A month later, her friend Jennifer Canavinno suggested a blind date with someone named David Feherty—a golfer.

"I didn't watch golf on TV," she says. "I've never played golf. But, during the British Open, Jennifer kept telling me I should turn on the television and look for him. I never did."

When Feherty returned from Scotland—the Open was played at St. Andrews that year—his friend Gary Knott suggested a double date: David and Anita; Gary and Jennifer. Feherty was still going through his divorce but beginning to wonder if a final agreement was ever going to be reached.

"Gary thought we'd be good for one another," Anita says. "Both divorced—or getting divorced—both with two sons, type A and type B personalities. The only thing he didn't count on was David showing up drunk."

They went to an Italian restaurant in Highland Park called Patrizzio's. David now remembers the evening lasting thirty minutes. Anita doesn't think it lasted that long.

"We made it from the bar to the table," she says. "We sat down, and David took his straw, stuck it in my drink, and drained it. I stood up and said, 'I'm sorry, but I have to go now'—and left."

As it turned out, Knott and Canavinno hadn't seen Feherty drain the drink. That night, Canavinno called Anita and asked, "Why did you leave so suddenly?"

Before she answered, Anita said, "Does your friend have AIDS?" Then she told her what had happened. That seemed to be the end of it. Except Knott called the next day, pleading with her to give Feherty one more chance.

"He said David felt terrible about what happened and promised if I'd give him another chance he'd show up sober. So, we decided the four of us would go to a baseball game."

And so, the two casual-at-most baseball fans went out to the park. The game didn't really matter to either of them. David's behavior did.

"He was trying so hard," Anita remembers. "He was sober and showed up early. During the game you could see he was *not* going to drink. I felt badly for him, so I finally said, 'Would you like a hot dog and a beer?' He looked at me like I had just saved his life."

After that, they began dating whenever David was in town, which wasn't that often because he was still trying to rescue his career—first on the PGA Tour in 1995 and then overseas in 1996.

By then, there were physical issues that had nothing to do with his drinking. He was having trouble with both elbows. The pain didn't stop him from playing, but he felt it on every swing. He played in twenty-six tournaments in 1995, poorly for the most part. He didn't have a top-ten finish all year and finished in the top twenty-five twice: a T-19 in February in Los Angeles and a T-11 at the International in August. His third-best finish was a T-31 at the Open, played that year at St. Andrews and won by another alcoholic, John Daly.

Feherty kept playing through all sorts of pain—physical and emotional—right to the end of the year, trying desperately to stay fully exempt. He missed twelve cuts, withdrew once, and was disqualified once. He finished T-65 in the Texas Open, the final event of the season, which left him 166th on the money list.

He went back to Q-school; the finals were played that year at Jack Nicklaus's course at Bear Lakes in Florida. Back then, the field was cut from 180 players to 90 players after the first four of the six rounds. He missed the four-round cut, which left him with no status at all for 1996.

"I wanted to keep playing," he says. "I needed to keep playing. I had no idea how else I could make a living. All I'd done since I was seventeen was play golf—that was twenty years at that point. I still had status in South Africa, so I played there in the winter, and I still had status in Europe as a past champion, so I played there."

He played twice in the United States—once in what was now his hometown event, the Byron Nelson Classic in Dallas—and in the International. In all, he played seventeen times in Europe and played well enough to finish ninety-second on the money list, which, as he points out, wasn't bad for a drunk who had trouble swinging the golf club because of pain in his elbows. He finished second once—his only top-ten finish.

But his life away from the golf course changed considerably after Anita came into his life. After they started dating seriously, she asked about his divorce agreement. When he showed her what had been agreed to, she was horrified.

"The lawyer he had hired was, for all intents and purposes, someone you hired if you got a traffic ticket," she says. "He had no idea what he was doing. Of course, neither did David. If he hadn't changed lawyers, he might not be divorced yet. It might still be going on. He needed a real lawyer."

Anita found one, Kathryn Murphy. It was difficult to undo a lot of what had already been agreed to, but she did get the divorce finalized with terms that were better than what had originally been proposed—and accepted.

Not long after his divorce was final, David began proposing to Anita. By then, she was traveling with him on occasion when he went to play in Europe. She made trips to Dubai, Sweden, Portugal, and Ireland. On one trip she brought all four boys—her two sons, who were twelve and ten at the time, and Shey and Rory, who were seven and three, respectively.

"He wanted me to meet all his mates," Anita remembers. "It was as if he wanted them to see that he was going to get it right the second time."

He also introduced her to his family. "Caroline was quite beautiful," David's mother remembers. "But she worked at it all the time. I thought Anita was naturally glamorous."

By then, Feherty was telling anyone who would listen that he was going to marry Anita—just as soon as she said yes to one of his proposals. One person who wasn't so sure that was a great idea was Torrance.

"I think he was a little bit nervous that David was talking about getting married again so soon given the way the first marriage had ended," Anita says.

Nowadays, Torrance, like everyone who cares about Feherty, is very much a member of the Anita fan club. He says the same thing about her that Feherty says: "She saved his life. If not for her, he wouldn't still be here."

Anita finally said yes to one of David's proposals when he came home from a trip to South Africa. By then, David was living in Anita's house, and the boys were there with him whenever he had them. The plan had been for him to walk in from the garage and dramatically drop to his knees and ask her to please marry him.

Except he didn't make it inside.

"I came to the door when he got home, and all of a sudden, he dropped to his knee still in the garage," Anita says. "At that point, how could I say no?"

And so, on May 31, 1996, they were married. In fairy tales, they would live happily ever after. They have lived with a good deal of happiness for twenty-seven years now, but their life has been a lot more complicated than a fairy tale.

CHAPTER FIVE

TV Finds Feherty

THE SECOND-MOST-IMPORTANT PERSON TO COME into Feherty's life in 1995 was Gary McCord.

McCord played full time on the PGA Tour for thirteen years. He was the classic "journeyman," playing well enough to remain fully exempt throughout that time but never winning a tournament. He finished second twice—both times in Milwaukee (1975 and 1977)—but didn't win until he got to the Senior Tour. He won twice on that tour in 1999. By then he was a TV star, having gone to work for CBS in 1986 at the age of thirty-seven.

Prior to that, McCord had played an important and largely unsung role in the development of the PGA Tour.

For years, only the top sixty players on the tour's season-ending money list were fully exempt for the next season. Those who made it through Q-school, which started in 1965, were eligible to play in Monday qualifiers each week along with those who finished out of the top sixty on the tour's money list the previous year.

They were known in those days as "rabbits," because they hopped from tour stop to tour stop, never guaranteed a spot in the next week's tournament unless they had qualified the previous week *and* made the cut.

McCord was a rabbit when he first came on tour in 1974. In the late 1970s, he began pushing the notion of what became known as "the all-exempt tour," and at the conclusion of the 1982 season, the PGA Tour decided it was a good idea, making the top 125 players on the money list fully exempt and making those who made it through Q-school fully exempt too—although they had to wait week to week to make certain each tournament had space available.

Monday qualifying continued to exist, but it was almost exclusively for non-tour members, with only four spots available each week. The Monday events became known as "four-spotters," as in, "How did he get into the field? He four-spotted."

When Feherty made it through Q-school in the United States in 1993 in a tie for eleventh place, he was a beneficiary of the all-exempt tour. If he had come to the United States prior to the start of the 1983 season, his success at Q-school would only have given him status as a rabbit—the same status he had during his first two years on the European Tour.

McCord's last full-time season on tour was 1986, when he played twenty-one times and made ten cuts. That was the year when Frank Chirkinian offered him a job at CBS. McCord didn't fit the profile of a typical pro-turned-talker, but he brought one thing to the network that was more or less unheard of in TV golf prior to his arrival: a sense of humor, a sometimes off-the-wall sense of humor.

"Not Feherty off the wall," he likes to point out. "But a little bit off the wall."

He quickly became popular with those who watched golf on TV because he would say things no one else would say and because he made the listener laugh, something that hadn't existed in the past in televised golf. The whispers one often heard from commentators in those days weren't just to be sure the players weren't distracted by hearing their voices; they were to make sure the viewer understood that what they were watching was important.

Chirkinian, who was executive producer of CBS's golf coverage for thirty-seven years, constantly railed at McCord during telecasts, but recognized that he had something unique and was willing to let McCord be McCord even when it created headaches for him.

The biggest one came in 1994 when McCord made two comments during the Masters that made the Lords of Augusta crazy. McCord was in the tower at seventeen and noted at one point that landing a second shot on the green and getting it to stop was almost impossible because "the greens look like they've been bikini-waxed."

The Lords didn't like anyone implying their greens were too fast, especially as graphically as calling them "bikini-waxed."

McCord also noted that if a shot didn't stay on the seventeenth green and rolled over it, the player had almost no chance to get up and down from there for par. "There are body bags back there," he said—again giving a description far more graphic than the Lords wished to hear.

These were people, it should be remembered, who once banned the great Jack Whitaker from CBS telecasts for five years because he referred to the fans—"patrons," in Augusta-speak—around the eighteenth green as a mob, not a mob that was going to burn anything down, but a lot of people. There are no mobs of any kind inside the hallowed gates of Augusta.

After the 1994 tournament, Augusta National, which has final say on all announcers for the Masters, demanded that McCord be removed from CBS's future coverage. Chirkinian had no choice but to go along but stood behind McCord and kept him on every other tournament CBS televised. For his part, McCord used Masters week to make lucrative speaking appearances, and would tell funny stories about his Augusta experiences.

After all, they couldn't ban him *again*.

A little more than a year later, another CBS announcer got into trouble, but this time it had nothing to do with the Masters and nothing to do with anything said on air. The network was televising the 1995 LPGA Championship, which was being played at DuPont Country Club in Wilmington, Delaware. Valerie Helmbreck, a reporter for the *Wilmington News-Journal,* did what would normally have been an innocent pre-tournament interview with Ben Wright, who had been working on golf tournaments for CBS since 1972. He had replaced the iconic British journalist/announcer Henry Long-hurst as CBS's "British voice."

McCord's presence on the telecasts had brought out Wright's sense of humor. "We just went at each other all the time," McCord says. "Ben was very funny, but I don't think viewers understood that until I got there and sort of gigged at him on air. People enjoyed it and so did we."

Sadly, there was nothing funny about Wright's interview with Helmbreck. Talking about why women's golf wasn't more popular, Wright said, "Let's face facts here. Lesbians in the sport are hurting women's golf."

He went on to say, "They're going to a butch game and that furthers the bad image of the game. . . . Women are handicapped by big boobs. It's not easy for them to keep the left arm straight and that's one of the tenets of the game. Their boobs get in the way."

Wright instantly denied the quotes, and CBS stood by him—as did the LPGA Tour. "I am convinced the offensive statements attributed to Mr. Wright were not made," CBS Sports president David Kenin said in a statement that week—not answering any follow-up questions.

The LPGA, which wanted as much TV attention as it could get, allowed the great Nancy Lopez to share a booth with Wright that weekend, which was a huge gesture of support for Wright and CBS. The only thing Helmbreck had on her side, as it turned out, was the truth.

Wright continued to work for CBS for the rest of the year. But over the next several months, it became more and more apparent that Wright's denials were lies. A part-time CBS employee told *Sports Illustrated* in a December story that he had overheard the interview and that Helmbreck had quoted Wright accurately.

In that same story, Dan Jenkins, the revered golf writer and a friend of Wright's, said Wright had told him at a party that he'd made the comments—noting that Wright had been drinking when he admitted to the truth of Helmbreck's reporting.

In January, the network felt it had no choice and pulled Wright from future telecasts—though technically he wasn't fired, because he had three years left on his contract. The first person to take Wright's place was Bobby Clampett.

"I went from two tournaments in 1995 to twenty in 1996," Clampett says. "At the end of '94, my agent told me CBS was going to give me a full schedule, so I didn't bother going to Q-school that year. Turned out I only got two tournaments. Then Ben got fired, and I got a full schedule."

Clampett had been a rising star on tour in the early 1980s— leading the British Open by seven shots during the third round in 1982 at the age of twenty-two before a triple bogey on the seventh hole at Royal Troon caused him to unravel and finish in a tie for tenth place the next day. Later that year, he won the Southern Open. But he never won again, settling into a solid midlevel career before CBS hired him as a part-time on-course reporter in 1991. He only got to work two tournaments in 1995 because CBS had lost NFL telecasts (to Fox) and was forced to move some of its football announcers to golf—notably Verne Lundquist—in order to give them enough work to justify what they were being paid.

"I was happy they hired me," Clampett says, laughing. "I was especially happy they hired a golfer and not another football announcer."

But even with Clampett installed, with Wright gone, CBS still needed a replacement "British" voice. American networks have always believed a British voice—or a voice with a non-American accent—is needed on golf telecasts. ABC had the great Peter Alliss; for years CBS had Longhurst and then Wright. NBC never had a British (or Irish) voice until it hired Feherty, but years earlier, Australian Bruce Devlin worked for the network.

It was McCord who found CBS's next non-American voice—by accident. He was in the locker room looking for players to interview during a first-round rain delay at the 1995 International when he heard uproarious laughter coming from around the corner. He peeked around and saw Feherty holding court.

"I'd never met him," McCord says. "I knew who he was because he'd been such a good player in Europe and had played in the '91 Ryder Cup. I stood there and listened for a while and realized he was fall-down funny. It wasn't as if he was working from a script or anything, he was just telling stories.

"As the delay was ending, I walked up and introduced myself. I knew the next day [Friday] was going to be a long day on-air because we weren't going to finish the first round that day, and at that event there was always the potential for more rain delays."

In fact, Jim Nantz says that rain delays were so prevalent at the International that planning for rain delays was part of the pre-tournament production meetings.

"I said, 'Look, if you feel like it tomorrow, when you're finished playing, come up to the tower at fifteen and sit with me for a while,'" McCord says. "'We could have some fun.'"

Feherty was scheduled to play early the next day and was pretty sure he was going to miss the cut. He was playing poorly and was in jeopardy of losing his full-time playing privileges on the US Tour at year's end.

"I wasn't really sure if I wanted to do it," Feherty says. "But Gary was very nice, and I figured, what the heck, I've got nothing better to do. It wasn't like working on my game after I played was going to help me at that point. If anything, it was probably just going to make me feel worse—physically and mentally."

McCord wasn't certain Feherty was going to show up, but he decided to give Chirkinian a heads-up that Feherty might join him. Chirkinian knew exactly who Feherty was and his reputation for having an out-of-the-box sense of humor.

"He said, 'Are you out of your fucking mind?'" McCord remembers, still laughing at the memory. "He's crazy! Last thing I need is you two crazy fucking Irishmen in there together."

"Come on, Frank," McCord said. "It's Friday, and it's cable [USA Network]. No one's watching anyway. It's going to be a long day. Let's try to have some fun."

As luck would have it, Feherty, having decided to take McCord up on his invitation, had just arrived and heard Chirkinian quite clearly.

"Frank didn't know I could hear every word he was saying," Feherty says. "But I was quite amused by it. I didn't think anything he said about me was wrong on any level."

When McCord told Chirkinian that Feherty was in the booth, he relented, and Feherty put on a headset.

"I think we were on for three hours that day," McCord says. "David wasn't just funny; he had insights you just didn't hear very often, if at all. He was crazy smart and kept me laughing the whole afternoon. He was brilliant."

As the two men went down the steps to leave the tower at the end of the telecast, McCord said to Feherty: "I don't know how much longer you're going to play. But whenever you're done, this is what you're going to do next. Please keep us [CBS] in mind when the time comes."

Feherty heard what McCord said but didn't take it that seriously. He had just turned thirty-seven and was still trying to rescue his golf career.

CHAPTER SIX

New Life

By the time 1995 ended, Feherty had a problem: he was madly in love with a woman who lived in Dallas; his two sons—ages seven and three—were living there, and he had no place to play in the United States.

"That period was tumultuous," Rory Feherty says. "Shey and I were living some of the time with our mother and some of the time with him and Anita. We were very much caught in between two very different points of view. Dad being away as much as he was made it that much harder."

Anita had been willing to go on that second date in July 1995 because she saw in Feherty what almost everyone in his life sees in him: "I guess, even though he was drunk, I saw a kindness in him, even that first night, even in just a few minutes," she says. "I think that's something people see in him because it's quite real. It's earned him a lot of mulligans in life."

The second date turned out to be the most important mulligan of Feherty's life. After their baseball game date, they began seeing each other regularly whenever David was in town, while Anita continued to run her successful home design business.

Having lost his playing privileges in the United States, Feherty spent most of 1996 playing in Europe. He was still exempt there as a five-time tournament winner. He also played in South Africa again during the winter, which meant he spent a lot of time on airplanes and overseas. There wasn't much point trying to fly home in between tournaments in Europe, so he stayed in Scotland with Sam and Suzanne Torrance and their family.

"I think when I think of my father when I was young, the first word that comes to my mind is absence," Rory Feherty says. "He was either gone playing golf or, later, gone commentating on golf. But when I felt as if I *really* needed him for something, he found a way to be there. That was his saving grace as far as I was concerned."

Feherty actually played reasonably well in Europe in '96—finishing ninety-second on the money list—but wasn't nearly the player he'd been before he was forced to move to the United States and before his drinking and the trouble he was having with both his elbows began to affect his game. What kept him going were trips back to Dallas when he got to see Anita and his boys. He and Caroline finally got divorced, which was a good news–bad news story.

"I was beginning to think the whole thing was never going to end," he says. "The day we finalized it, I jumped over my lawyer's desk I was so happy. But she [Caroline] took me for pretty much everything because I was willing to sign just about anything to get it over with, although the deal we finally made was better than the one I had initially agreed to with my first lawyer. As it was, I ended up with the two boys part time and a car. For a while, we lived in a two-bedroom apartment that looked like a room at the Marriott. Eventually, we moved in with Anita."

One of Feherty's best tournaments in '96 had come in South Africa, and it had qualified him to play in the World Series of Golf in Akron in August of that year. By then, he and Anita were married, and he was deciding what to do next with his life, since playing in Europe was no longer an option when he was living in Dallas with a wife and four kids and he had no playing status in the United States.

He was sitting in the hotel bar in Akron, the site of the World Series of Golf, when he saw two men walking in his direction: Rick Gentile and Lance Barrow, both from CBS. McCord had told him it was possible CBS might approach him about doing some work for the network. At the time, Gentile was CBS's executive vice president for programming and Barrow was about to succeed Chirkinian as the executive producer of CBS's golf telecasts.

"I was drinking vodka and Gatorade because, after all, I was an athlete," Feherty says, laughing. "These two guys came up and said they were from CBS. At that moment, I completely forgot about McCord telling me CBS might be interested in hiring me. My first thought, honest to God, was 'They're from *60 Minutes* and they're doing a piece on athletes and alcohol and drugs and they want to talk to me.' I was looking for a way to get out, but there was none. So, I talked to them."

Gentile's memory is that he and Barrow had made an appointment to meet Feherty, but it is entirely possible—all parties agree—that Feherty had forgotten. They sat in a corner of the bar and Gentile and Barrow told Feherty they were interested in giving him a tryout on air. Both sides had one concern: Feherty's drinking.

"We were certainly aware of it," Gentile says. "We brought it up to him. He was very honest. He never said it wasn't an issue or it was something he knew he could kick in a few weeks. He said, 'The one thing I'll tell you is this: I never drink when I'm working. And if I come to work for you, I won't drink before I'm on air.' There was something about the way he said it that made me believe him."

Feherty's concern wasn't so much whether he could stay sober when working but whether he could be funny when he was sober. "By then I was so used to drinking and being funny, I wondered if I could *not* drink and still be funny. I knew they were interested in me because I had an Irish accent and because I was funny or, at least, was supposed to be funny. The accent wasn't a problem. Being funny was the concern—for them and for me."

Gentile was convinced that Feherty and McCord on air together would bring an entirely different sound to golf on TV. Pat Summerall had just left the network to move to Fox in order to continue doing NFL football and Jim Nantz had replaced him on the tower at eighteen. That meant Nantz's input about who CBS would hire was important.

"I remember talking to Jim about whether we should approach Feherty," Gentile says. "He was very enthusiastic. In fact, he said to me, 'You guys need to go after him before another network grabs him.'"

Nantz remembers being pro-Feherty, but thinks Gentile is giving him too much credit. "I was all for it," he says. "I knew who he was because he was a good player in Europe, because of the '91 Ryder Cup, and because people knew he had once been an aspiring opera singer, which certainly made him different. But Gary's the one who pushed it. Gary's the one who deserves the credit. Gary and Rick and Lance. I did think it was a really good idea, but I'm not the one who first thought of it."

There was one other person who had pushed Feherty to the network: Tom Watson. This was a twist because the ever-serious Watson was not a fan of McCord's. In fact, he had written Chirkinian a note after the infamous 1994 Masters, backing up the position of the Lords that McCord didn't belong on the air at Augusta.

He barely knew Feherty at the time but enjoyed his sense of humor.

"David was different," Watson says. "I can't even tell you exactly where I'd heard him, whether he was speaking somewhere or if it was just in the locker room. I didn't know him at all back then, but I thought he was funny. I liked his brand of irreverence. I told Frank Chirkinian he should consider hiring him. Little did I know they were already thinking about him."

Nantz had done a piece on Feherty for CBS's *New Breed* series, a Chirkinian invention created to introduce young players to the golf audience. Feherty was thirty-five when he came to the United States, so he didn't exactly fit the *New Breed* profile. But his biography was so different Chirkinian and Nantz decided to do the piece anyway.

Barrow, who was Chirkinian's number one lieutenant at the time, worked on the piece with Nantz. "I remember him being remarkably smart and funny," Barrow says. "But what I remember most is him saying he wouldn't play golf past the age of forty. No one ever said that, even back then. This was when he was still playing very well."

Feherty had always been consistent with that thought. When he first arrived on the European Tour, he told Sam Torrance he didn't expect to play beyond forty. "Can't explain why I said it or thought it," he says. "But I always felt that way. I just knew I wasn't going to be playing golf for a living in my forties."

After the Akron meeting, Gentile and Barrow ended up offering Feherty a three-tournament tryout deal. Both wanted to see him on air—sober—and how he would interact with the network's other announcers: Nantz, Ken Venturi, Clampett, Lundquist, Peter Kostis, McCord, and another new hire, Peter Oosterhuis.

"He fit in from day one," Clampett says. "Everyone liked him because how do you not like David Feherty? He was funny, and he had no ego. He got along with everyone, which wasn't always the case for us in those days."

In fact, there was always some tension within the CBS ranks back then. According to Clampett, Kostis and McCord didn't get along especially well with Venturi. Nantz always got along with everyone, and Feherty and Clampett often had to calm the waters between McCord-Kostis and Venturi.

CBS Sports had been in a state of upheaval since it had lost the NFL. "At one point we had four different executive producers for different sports," Nantz remembers. "That was unheard of. When Fox got the NFL, we lost people left and right, most notably James Brown, Pat [Summerall], and John [Madden] in front of the camera. We also lost five important producers, including Ed Goren, who was our number one NFL producer.

"David was a perfect fit for the golf group. We'd had a lot of changes just prior to that: Pat leaving, me moving to eighteen, Ben being gone, and Verne becoming a regular part of the team. Kostis was the first swing teacher ever hired by a network. Oosterhuis had just joined us. Almost no one was in the same role he had been in a few years earlier. David made the telecasts better, but he also made everyone's off-air life a little better. In his own way, he was a calming influence."

"For a while during those early days I felt like I was some kind of glue," Feherty says. "Ken really didn't like McCord and Kostis. He didn't think they were traditional enough—especially McCord. He also missed Summerall; they worked well on the air, and they were drinking partners off it. I got along with Gary and Peter right away, and I drank with Venturi. He liked that about me."

The other change—a significant one—was Barrow replacing Chirkinian as the executive producer at the end of 1996. Chirkinian was known as "the Ayatollah" because he ruled CBS's golf coverage with an iron hand for thirty-seven years. He was also known as "the Father of Televised Golf," a title bestowed on him for his many innovations, including inventing the concept of reporting scores relative to par, as opposed to cumulative score. That allowed the viewer to understand more clearly exactly who stood where on a leaderboard.

CBS was ready to "retire" Chirkinian at the end of 1995. It was Nantz who talked the network out of that decision. "I remember being at 'the Shark Shootout,' and I just picked up a phone and called Peter Lund [who was the CEO of sports at the network at the time]," he says. "I said, 'You can't do this to Frank Chirkinian. You have to at least give him a farewell tour.'"

CBS did give Chirkinian an extra year, so he was still around when the decision was made to approach Feherty. In spite of his initial misgivings at the International a year earlier, Chirkinian was all in on the idea of hiring Feherty. "He pulled me aside at one point and said, 'Putting Feherty in the tower that day was a genius idea,'" McCord remembers. "Coming from Frank, that was a big deal."

Feherty worked with Chirkinian only a couple of times—notably on the "PGA Grand Slam of Golf," which was a four-man exhibition televised in the fall by TNT that included that year's major champions or alternates. By the time Feherty worked his first Masters for CBS—Tiger Woods's breakout twelve-shot victory in 1997—Barrow was in charge.

After his three-tournament tryout, CBS offered him a three-year contract for $300,000 a year. The most important thing about the new job was that it allowed him to work exclusively in the United States and, frequently, in places where he could get home to Dallas on Sunday night.

CBS smartly decided early on that Feherty would do his best work "on the ground," the TV term for having someone walk with a group rather than sit in a tower and describe what they are seeing in a monitor.

"Sometimes you get lucky," Barrow says. "Fact is, we didn't have a tower to put him in when we hired him. Jim and Kenny were at eighteen; we'd hired Oosterhuis to take Ben's place at seventeen, and Gary was at fifteen. When we did regular tournaments, we had Clampett at sixteen—except at the Masters when Verne [Lundquist] was at sixteen and Bobby was at Amen Corner. The only logical place for him was on the ground. Turned out that was exactly where he belonged."

The idea to have someone follow players "on the ground" had originated in the mid-1970s when ABC hired past PGA champion Bob Rosburg to walk the golf course with key groups and, most often, the final group. Judy Rankin followed soon after as an on-course reporter, and the two of them changed the way golf was televised by getting much closer to the players while they were play-ing than anyone had gotten in the past.

Rosburg became an iconic figure in golf for his blunt assessments of what a player faced after hitting a poor shot. "That one's dead, Jim"—a comment directed at Jim McKay in the eighteenth-hole tower—became a phrase golfers at every level used to describe dire situations.

Eventually, the other networks followed ABC's lead. Kostis was working on the ground for CBS when Feherty arrived, and rather than put Feherty in a tower, Barrow opted to have him follow the last group most of the time on Saturdays and Sundays.

Right from the start, it worked.

"I always had a thing with Ben [Wright] where we would go back and forth at one another," McCord says. "But we were both working in towers. With David on the ground, it was different. I could ask him a question about what was going on down there, and he could answer me, often quite sharply." ("What do you think's going on, Gary? He's up against a tree, and I don't think the tree is inclined to move.")

Beyond that, Feherty's style was different than anyone had ever seen or heard on network television. Clampett remembers asking him early on about a lie Davis Love III had after he had badly missed the fifteenth green during the tournament at Westchester. "I don't want to say the rough is deep in here," Feherty said. "But I think my shoelaces are mating down there."

When Feherty's hero, Lee Trevino, hit a shot off-line during a Senior Slam event in Mexico, Clampett said, "Where'd that one end up, David?"

To which Feherty replied, "I think it's over there in some heavily armed Mexican vegetables."

Later in that same event, after an Isao Aoki chip-in, TNT producer Ken Nolin asked Feherty to demonstrate the shot. Because it was
an exhibition, the rules about what announcers could and could not
do were different. Feherty was carrying a wedge and went to the spot
where Aoki had chipped in from, tossed a ball down, and promptly
shanked it off a golf cart. Without missing a beat, he turned to the
camera and said, "And now you know why I don't play on tour
anymore."

In the fall of 1996, while still learning on the job, Feherty worked
with Clampett at the so-called PGA Grand Slam of Golf in Hawaii.
Nick Faldo had won the Masters that year—his last major title.
When he three-putted the third hole from seventy feet on day one
of the thirty-six-hole event, Nolin suggested that Feherty putt from
the spot where Faldo's ball had been to show people how difficult
the putt had been.

Feherty holed the putt.

"Only time—and I mean the only time—I've ever seen David
speechless," Clampett says, laughing.

As luck would have it, Feherty arrived at CBS at the same time
Tiger Woods became Tiger Woods. Woods had won twice in the
fall of 1996 as a twenty-year-old tour rookie. His remarkable arrival
and ascent sent the entire golf world—the entire sports world
really—into a fever that was quickly labeled "Tiger-mania."

Sports Illustrated named Woods its Sportsman of the Year at
the end of 1996, causing *New York Daily News* columnist Mike
Lupica to quip that Woods was the first athlete to win the award
"on spec."

Feherty's first Masters for CBS was in 1997, the year a twenty-
one-year-old Woods turned spec into reality and won the tournament
by twelve shots. His performance was perhaps best summed up by

Tom Watson—who finished tied for second. "He's a boy among men," Watson said. "And he's showing the men how to do it."

From that moment on Woods became golf's transcendent figure. "He doesn't move the needle," ESPN's Tony Kornheiser would often say. "He *is* the needle."

Then, as now, CBS televised two of golf's four major tournaments—the Masters and the PGA Championship—and also televised more of the week-to-week events than anyone else. Woods was frequently in the last group and the announcer assigned to walk with the last group was Feherty.

To say that Woods was as opaque as any star athlete on the planet is a vast understatement. He had been taught by his father to trust no one; to give away nothing for free; and to be suspicious of anyone carrying a notebook, a tape recorder, or a microphone. Woods was the absolute master of the Andrea Kirby/Crash Davis nonanswer. Even his on-camera smiles felt and looked rehearsed.

When he was asked if he was turning pro after winning a third straight US Amateur, Woods answered, "I really don't know."

IMG already had contracts in place for him and Nike was ready to release its first "Woods" commercial the day he turned pro.

But Woods couldn't resist Feherty. "I think part of it was he knew how much I respected his game and the shots he was creating," Feherty says. "Some of the things I said were funny, but a lot of things I said were just me responding to what he was doing. Plus, I think he understood that I didn't want anything from him. I just wanted to describe as best I could what he was doing out there. And to try to have fun."

Woods delighted in overhearing Feherty give his version of "That one's dead, Jim" when he had a seemingly impossible shot. "Watch this one, Farty," he would say just before he pulled off the shot.

It wasn't as if Feherty and Woods became regular dinner companions or even dinner companions at all. But Woods was clearly comfortable with Feherty, even occasionally telling him off-color jokes when he knew he couldn't be heard.

"He would actually pull his cap down low over his face so that no one could read his lips," Feherty says. "And then he'd tell me a joke."

One that Feherty likes to retell during his stand-up routine went like this:

"Hey, Farty, do you know what you call a Black guy flying an airplane?"

"No, Tiger, I don't. What do you call him?"

"A pilot, you fucking racist."

Woods loves to tell jokes like that, and jokes considerably dirtier than that, and in Feherty—or, as he liked to call him, "Farty"—he found an appreciative audience. He also found someone willing to take part in farting contests with him. Feherty loves bathroom humor. So does Woods. Once, a microphone picked up a rather distinctive fart when Woods was on camera, and it was attributed by mistake to Woods, causing a minor media sensation. Feherty had to come to the rescue by saying *he* had farted into the microphone. Woods just happened to be on camera at that moment.

Feherty's penchant for farting did get him into trouble once. It was during the third round in Charlotte at the Wells Fargo Championship. Feherty was walking with Woods's group. Barrow always liked to confirm that his announcers knew CBS was coming back from commercial. He would do a quick whip around in the thirty seconds prior to coming back on.

"It would go something like, 'Nantz? Here. McCord? Yup. Ian? Yes, sir. And, Feherty?'" McCord says. "The response was often a fart. On this day though, David got more than he bargained for."

Put simply, in searing heat, Feherty's response was, well, more than a fart. McCord knew what had happened right away. "They were on sixteen," he remembers. "As they walked to seventeen, I could see David had rain pants on. It was 100 degrees out and he was wearing rain pants."

Feherty flatly denies that he was wearing rain pants. The rest of the story, he concedes, is true.

"I was in rough shape," he says. "All I wanted to do was get to the clubhouse and get out of those pants. Naturally, the last two holes took forever. The guys finished, and I was ready to *run* to the clubhouse. Then Lance said, 'David, we're going to break. We need you to talk to Tiger when we come back.'"

Woods had played well enough that he was willing to talk, and he was always more likely to be a reasonably good interview if Feherty was asking the questions. The two men stood behind the eighteenth green waiting for the break to end and for Nantz to wrap up the third round before throwing to Feherty to talk to Woods.

Not surprisingly, Woods was getting antsy, having just played eighteen holes in searing heat. Feherty was beyond antsy. "I was dying," he says.

Woods finally looked at Feherty and said, "Are we doing this?" Before Feherty could answer, he added, "Did you just fart?"

"Technically, no," Feherty answered, to which Woods said, "Man, you've got to clean yourself up."

"I'm *not* sure if I'm finished yet," Feherty replied. Woods threw up his hands and said, "I'm going."

Feherty, hearing Nantz throwing to him (live) reached out with his hand and corralled Woods just enough to keep him on camera. "He was standing as far away from me as he could be and still be on camera," Feherty says. "We got through it—barely. As soon as I threw back to Nantz, he *ran*."

So did Feherty: inside to find relief.

Everyone had a laugh when it was over, no one more than McCord. He and Feherty had quickly become good friends and on-air partners in comedy. They were different: McCord tended to be more scripted; Feherty was completely unscripted. It worked.

"The fact that we liked each other was important," McCord says. "I think viewers can tell when people are forcing humor or trying to make it sound like they like one another when they don't, and they can tell when they actually *do* like one another. What made David a star so quickly was that everyone liked him: the people he worked with at CBS and the players. Even though he talked as if he'd never known which end of the golf club to hold, players knew better; they knew he'd been very good and that he knew what he was talking about when it came to golf."

Perhaps no group of athletes in the world is more spoiled or sensitive when it comes to being criticized—especially by former players on TV. For years, when Johnny Miller was NBC's number one analyst, players screamed loud and long about his occasional criticisms. The fact that he talked about "choking"—or, as the players call it, "the c-word"—put many players over the edge.

Years ago, during lunch in the players' dining room in Atlanta, several midlevel tour players were complaining loudly about Miller. "Where the hell does he come off criticizing *us*?" one said. "What did he ever do?"

When someone (me) pointed out to the group that Miller had won twenty-one times on the PGA Tour, including two major championships, they were all silent for a moment. "Really?" another in the group finally said. "Twenty-one wins? Maybe he does know what he's talking about."

"Yeah, but he still shouldn't say we choke," said the third player at the table.

Of course, all golfers choke; all *athletes* choke. Some just do it less than others and some—like Woods—almost never do it. Feherty never used "the c-word" on air, but he willingly pointed out poor shots and, at least as often, poor decisions. He also laughed at himself when he would do his own version of Rosburg's "That one's dead, Jim" on Woods only to watch him somehow extricate himself from jail. This happened consistently because Woods was often a wild driver of the golf ball but had a unique knack for finding the green from impossible spots.

"Whenever he looked at me before an impossible shot and said, 'Watch this one, Farty,' I knew I was in trouble," Feherty says. "Almost every time, the little SOB would pull off a shot I'd never seen before. If you ask me the fifty greatest shots I've ever seen, he probably hit forty-nine of them."

Feherty's star rose quickly at CBS. In addition to having him work at tournaments, CBS started a late-night show during golf season that he and McCord co-hosted. It was, to say the least, completely off the wall.

"You can't make someone into a good announcer or a great announcer," Barrow says. "They either have it or they don't. Different guys bring different skills to the table. Most people focus on David's humor, and that's accurate. But it was more than that: he understood the game and the golf swing. He also knew the rules as well as anyone I've ever met.

"Every lineup has to have a clean-up hitter, and it has to have a really good hitter in the middle of the lineup. That doesn't mean the other guys in the lineup aren't important—they are. But David was a middle-of-the-lineup guy right from the start. He was too good not to be."

The CBS people weren't the only ones who noticed. "When you cover a sport, you watch everyone who is televising that sport," says Dan Hicks, who has worked on NBC's golf telecasts for thirty years, the last twenty-two in the eighteenth-hole tower. "Naturally, I watched CBS whenever they had a tournament.

"I didn't know David personally at that point, but when I started listening to him on air, he just jumped off the screen. His humor was so different, different even than McCord's. And the two of them together was like nothing else any of us had ever heard on a golf telecast."

Veteran NBC sportscaster Jimmy Roberts didn't know Feherty either. He remembered him as part of the European Ryder Cup team in 1991 but knew nothing of his humor. "It was just *so* different, right from the start," he says. "And then, when I got to know him, I realized—I still realize—that there's never been anyone like him. No one.

"I know this is grammatically incorrect, but David is entirely unique. You can't *be* entirely unique but that's what David is."

Barrow was a different personality in the truck than Chirkinian. Although he had learned from Chirkinian and was a disciple, he rarely lectured his on-air talent during a telecast. "My job was to make sure the microphones worked and that they were all there with microphones turned on when they were supposed to be there," he says, laughing. "In the case of Feherty and McCord, I said the same thing to them before every broadcast: 'Don't say anything that gets you fired or anything that gets me fired.'"

After his first year at CBS, Feherty was locked in as a star. "I honestly don't know how much money I made or how much money I make now," he says. "My agent [Andy Elkin] and Anita handle everything. I've never negotiated a contract and, since I married Anita, I've never looked at or paid a bill. I just show up where and when they tell me to show up."

Early on, Feherty was also assigned to work on occasional women's tournaments that CBS televised. He never got into trouble the way Wright did, but he did have some issues: one that was his fault, one that wasn't. During a telecast of an LPGA event, Feherty, who is easily bored, was bored. And so, late in an early round telecast, he looked up from the tower and saw a threesome heading his way.

"Coming to you, David," he heard in his ear.

Without thinking or looking to see who might be in the threesome, he said, "Well, here come three more big women I don't recognize."

He had to apologize for that comment and had to endure a stern lecture from his bosses in New York. But he survived. That might have been an example of the "mulligans" Anita talks about him getting for the simple reason that people like him.

"I'm pretty sure I wouldn't have survived that comment in today's world," he says. "I'm pretty sure there are others who might not have survived it back then. I did. I was lucky."

The second incident wasn't his fault. In fact, it was no one's fault. One could even say it was a moment of social progress. CBS was televising an LPGA event from Daytona Beach. It was the first year CBS had televised the event, and it was being played at a new golf club, one that didn't even have a clubhouse yet. Almost inevitably, there was a rain delay. There were no highlights to show from the previous year because the tournament hadn't been on TV, and there was no clubhouse to send a camera to for player interviews. The players were hiding out in their cars to try to stay dry.

"Tell you what," Barrow said to Feherty. "Go find Patty Sheehan and ask her what a Hall of Famer does to pass the time during a rain delay like this one."

Sheehan had been inducted into the World Golf Hall of Fame in 1993 and had won thirty-five times on the LPGA Tour—including six major championships.

Feherty complied with Barrow's directive, walking through the parking lot with a camera crew until he found Sheehan's car. Feherty tapped on the window and Sheehan rolled it down. All good. Feherty, microphone in hand, cameraman directly behind him said, "So, Patty, how does a member of the World Golf Hall of Fame kill time during a rain delay like this one?"

Without missing a beat, Sheehan nodded at the woman sitting in the car with her and said, "Rebecca and I are sitting here looking at baby pictures. We've decided to adopt."

At that moment, Feherty heard Barrow saying, "Thank her and throw it back to [Bill] Macatee. Bill, take us to break. Right now!"

Recalling the moment now, Barrow laughs. "I sent David to talk to Patty not just because she was such a great player but because she was always so great with the media and so easy for all of us to work with," he says. "Maybe if David had been a little more experienced, I would have told him to say, 'Do you have any names picked out?' But he wasn't and, of course, the answer *did* catch us off guard. So, I told him to throw it to Bill right away."

For the record, Sheehan and Rebecca Gaston have two children.

Feherty admits he was completely stunned by the answer. "Once we were off camera, I said to Patty, 'What the fuck was that?'" he says. "I just never figured she would pick that moment to come out. She thought it was hysterical. Looking back, I guess it was."

It was soon after the Sheehan interview that all CBS announcers and producers were summoned to "Black Rock"—CBS's headquarters in New York—for a daylong seminar on, as Clampett puts it, "Being careful."

It had been almost ten years since Jimmy "the Greek" Snyder's infamous comments claiming that Blacks were better athletes than Whites because slave owners had bred slaves to produce bigger, stronger offspring. Years later had come the Ben Wright incident, and then there had been Sheehan's coming out on camera, which nowadays certainly wouldn't be major or controversial news.

"They brought in a woman from what would now be called HR, I guess," Clampett says. "She basically lectured us on being careful not to say anything the least bit controversial. If I remember correctly, David brought a blanket and pillow and slept through most of it."

"I think I did sleep through most of it," Feherty remembers. "It was a little like being told, 'Look both ways before you cross the street.' She talked to us like we were a bunch of children."

As much as he enjoyed working for CBS, life still wasn't easy for Feherty. He and Anita had gotten married in May 1996 and in June 1998 had a daughter, Erin, to go with the four older boys they'd had in their previous marriages. The marriage was happy most of the time, but Feherty still struggled with addiction and depression. He was sober for a while and then not sober. There were times when Anita came home and found him drinking.

"She never directly threatened to leave me back then," he says. "But she said the drinking was unacceptable, and she might move out until I got sober in order to protect Erin. I had to do something about it, especially with a very young daughter we were raising together. What usually got me sober was the fear of her leaving me."

Erin Feherty is twenty-five now, has a degree from the University of Oklahoma, and is living in Los Angeles. In 2022, she left her job with an advertising agency to become a production assistant on a start-up situation comedy. She remembers being extremely aware of her father's struggles with addiction.

"Not when I was very young," she says. "But as I got older, I realized there were times when he was sober and times when he wasn't. It was toughest, I think, on my mother. She was always the one who had to hold things together."

According to Rory Feherty, it was also tough on Erin's two older brothers but in a different way. "We were back and forth between two homes," he says. "Anita's a very strong woman—she has to be. When we were young, we thought she was very stern. Our mother was far more lax. It was only when we got older that we realized that Anita had to be tough to keep things together—for my dad and for us."

It wasn't as if Feherty didn't try. The one time he went away to rehab—in 2016—he lasted twelve days. "I simply couldn't do it," he says. "I'm just not good dealing with people in groups, especially people I don't know. I think the end for me was when they gave me what they called an adult coloring book to work on. I just left. The place was killing me. If I had stayed, I might not have survived—literally."

When asked to describe an adult coloring book, Feherty says, "It's a coloring book."

His weight ballooned in the early 2000s, getting to as much as 245 pounds, close to 100 pounds more than he weighed when he first met Anita. "That had been much too little, the 245 was way too much," he says. "I still remember Erin climbing on to my lap one night when she was a toddler. I had an empty whiskey bottle sitting there, and she said, 'Daddy, I guess you need another bottle.' To this day, I can still hear her saying that. I'm not saying it was a wake-up call—I'd had plenty of them in my life—but it certainly resonated with me at the time."

For the first ten years he worked at CBS, Feherty continued to battle his addictions and his depression issues—although the latter had yet to be diagnosed. He was a star, but he was still struggling. On a vacation trip to the Bahamas in 2006, he got alcohol poisoning.

"I was good on TV in those days," he says. "I wasn't so good off TV. It's a miracle that Anita stuck with me through those years."

Anita remembers that trip vividly. "He warned me on the way down," she says. "It was a vacation, and he said, 'Look, I'm going to be with my mates, and I'm going to have a good time.' That meant he was going to drink. He had stopped drinking two years earlier when I'd finally threatened to leave him because Erin was getting to the age where she was starting to understand what was going on.

"But when he started again that weekend, he dove back in and started drinking as much as he'd been drinking before he had stopped. Naturally, his body couldn't take it. He ended up having a seizure in the shower. Couldn't get out of it."

One of those on the trip was Sam Torrance, who had never thought of Feherty's drinking as a major issue when they were traveling together on the European Tour. It was Torrance who came to the Fehertys' room to try to help Anita—getting Feherty out of the shower and trying to get him warm.

"I think that was an eye-opener for Sam," Anita says. "He'd never seen him like that."

When they got home, Anita found a substance abuse therapist named Mary Ann Watson to work with her husband.

But the real turning point came later that year, in the summer of 2006, with another Watson (no relation). Feherty was very much in demand by then to work non-CBS events, specifically exhibition matches that were syndicated. Tom Watson and Jack Nicklaus were playing one of those matches on Prince Edward Island in Canada. Feherty was asked by the producers to be the play-by-play announcer and the analyst, à la Jack Whitaker on *Shell's Wonderful World of Golf*—2.0. The day before the match was scheduled to be played, he interviewed both players for on-camera cut-ins that could be used while the match was being played.

Watson didn't actually know Feherty all that well. He'd never played with him when Feherty was still active, and he had never really socialized with him. But he had always thought he was funny and smart and liked listening to him do golf on television. "He had a way of being irreverent without being disrespectful," he says. "I liked that," which was why he had recommended Feherty to Frank Chirkinian ten years earlier.

At one point, during a lull in the taped prematch interview, Watson looked Feherty in the eye and said: "You're not well, are you?"

Feherty was caught off guard by the question. "He was giving me that Watson stare that he gives people when he's trying to make a point," he says. "I knew right away I wasn't going to be able to joke my way around what he was asking."

Watson had gone through his own battle with alcoholism, so what he was seeing that day wasn't unfamiliar to him.

"I felt like I was looking in a mirror, seeing exactly the same person I had been a few years earlier," he says. "I knew where he was and how he was feeling. It was easy to see he was in rough shape. I wanted to help if I could."

Watson told Feherty he knew an Alcoholics Anonymous group in Kansas City that he thought could help him, and they could put him in touch with an AA group in Dallas that could also help. Feherty was uncertain.

"I've never been good in groups," he says. "That's why I didn't do well in rehab. I had the same problem with the notion of being in an AA group."

Anita is more blunt: "He's good in groups where he's comfortable and feels in control," she says. "Definitely not in groups where he's not in control. Rehab was a disaster for him because he wouldn't even try to make it work. The people there told me, 'We can only help someone if they're willing to be helped.' David wasn't willing to be helped.'"

As Watson gave him the stare, Feherty stalled.

"Well, maybe after I get home, I'll get in touch with you," he said to Watson.

Watson knew a stall tactic when he heard it. He wanted Feherty to cancel his travel plans back to Dallas and fly with him to Kansas City, even if it would mean changing planes a couple times to get there.

Feherty still wasn't eager. "Sounds like it will be awfully difficult just to get there," he said.

That's when Nicklaus jumped in. "I've got a plane here," he said. "I can fly you both to Kansas City when the match is over."

Watson and Nicklaus had actually discussed confronting Feherty before Watson said anything to him. In truth, the whole thing was a setup. "We both knew and liked David," Watson says. "We both could see very clearly that he was sick, in rough shape. Jack knew what I was going to say when I said it, so when David tried to use the plane as an excuse, he was ready."

"I was out of excuses," Feherty says, laughing at the memory years later. "Tom and Jack both made it clear they weren't taking no for an answer. I realized I was being bullied by Tom Watson and kidnapped by Jack Nicklaus. I really didn't have a choice in the matter."

Nicklaus still remembers the day well. "I'd known David for a while by then, and I really liked him," he says. "I couldn't understand what he was going through the way Tom could, but I could see he wasn't well. He hadn't been well for a while. That was no secret. I figured anything I could do to help, I'd do."

After the match—which Nicklaus won—Nicklaus flew Watson and Feherty to Kansas City, the plane stopping in Columbus to drop Nicklaus off. Watson took Feherty to his AA group for several days and the people there recommended an AA group in Dallas they thought could help Feherty. It did—for a while.

"Looking back now, it was definitely better than rehab," he says. "Plus, Tom became my unofficial sponsor and counselor, which was probably the most important part of the whole thing. I probably talked to him more than I talked to the people at AA. Certainly, that was the case long term. He was a very good listener, and when *he* said something, I listened. I can tell you one thing: he didn't coddle me, which is exactly what I needed. I needed to be told when I was full of it."

What is fascinating about Feherty is how introverted he is in real life. When people meet him, they think he's an extrovert. When strangers approach him, whether at the golf course or in a restaurant or on the street, Feherty acts as if he has just run into a long-lost friend. He signs any autographs he is asked to sign, takes selfies forever, and laughs at every funny story he's told.

"Let me tell you about the time . . ."

Feherty reacts as if they are all beyond hilarious. Most of the time he says, "No, is that really true?" as if amazed by what he's hearing.

And the thrilled storyteller will tell him that yes, it is *absolutely* true.

"People come up to us in airports or in restaurants all the time," Erin Feherty says. "Sometimes, they'll just hand me their phone and say, 'Please take a picture of us.' I'm a lot like my dad, and there are times when I just want to say, 'Enough of this.' He never blinks. He's always gracious, which I know isn't always easy."

"He's the life of the party when people come up to him," Rory Feherty says. "And the funny thing is, he'd be very happy if he wasn't even at the party."

Feherty doesn't believe he deserves any kudos for being nice to strangers.

"Let's be honest, I'm where I am today because people like me," he says. "Plus, they're going out of their way to tell me that they like me and, in a lot of cases, why they like me. Why would I be rude? Would I rather eat in a restaurant and not be recognized? Sure. But when that day comes, it'll probably mean my value to anyone on TV or to my stand-up or as a speaker is long gone. I'm grateful that people want to come up and talk to me even if it isn't something I look forward to dealing with. In a way, it's part of my job."

The number of celebrities that take that approach to their obligation to the public can be counted in less than a minute.

As much as he understands how fortunate he is to be so popular, and as much as he enjoys—and is terrified—by his work, Feherty would be the first to tell you there is a very dark side to his life.

"I take thirteen pills a day, every day," he says. "They are for many different things. There are pills to help me deal with depression; pills that help me deal with being bipolar; there are pills for my ADD; pills to help me sleep; pills to help me with hypertension.

"There isn't a day that goes by when I'm not sad at some point. It's been that way pretty much all my life. I fight a constant fight to keep being sad from becoming depressed. It isn't always easy."

When he's home, Anita can recognize when he's going to, as she puts it, "a dark place." She will insist that the two of them go out somewhere—anywhere—to get him away from his dark thoughts. "He will always insist that he doesn't want to go, that he's fine, and I usually end up having to make him go," she says. "We'll go out somewhere, have lunch, do something, and when we get home, he'll say, 'Thanks for making me go.' Sometimes I have to remind him of that when he's insisting he doesn't want to go."

His depression issues started, he believes, when his teachers made him feel "worthless" in school because his undiagnosed ADD made it difficult, more often than not, for him to focus. It was no doubt exacerbated by the Troubles, which he now understands affected him more than he thought at the time.

"Because it was worse in other places than where we lived and because all the checkpoints, all the 'you can't go there' warnings and the bombings that we heard about that almost became part of daily life, there was a tendency to just go about your life as if this was a normal way to live," he says. "I do remember feeling scared at times when my dad was still working on the docks because things *did* happen down in that area of Belfast.

"But my mom was never one for sitting around and worrying. There really wasn't much point to it. There wasn't much of anything we could do. We just lived our lives as if what was going on was normal—which, for all of us, it was. But there was really nothing normal about it."

Trying to become a golf pro with a 5-handicap didn't do wonders for his self-belief either. Even when he did become a good player and did become successful, he still doubted himself. He knew he was drinking too much, and he knew he was an addict. Even though he can joke now about how difficult Caroline was to deal with, he still thinks he failed as a husband—and as a father.

"When a marriage doesn't work," he says now, "it's usually a team effort."

Feherty's life changed radically when he first went to work for CBS. He says repeatedly that Anita "saved my life," but there's no doubt that finding success after he could no longer succeed as a golfer was also vitally important.

"It wasn't just about having money, though that was certainly a good thing," he says. "It was about feeling I was good at something. I knew right from the start I was good at TV, that I could do it well. I *did* worry about whether I could be funny on air while I was sober, and I found out quickly that, not only could I do it, but I *enjoyed* it.

"When I was still playing, golf was work. It was my job and I always felt I had to work at it constantly to be competitive. But TV was never that way. It was fun and it was easy for me.

"A lot of that was Gary. I always knew I could engage with him and it would be good television. But I got on with everyone—Nantz, Kenny [Venturi], [Bobby] Clampett, Verne [Lundquist], Peter [Oosterhuis], Peter [Kostis], Ian [Baker-Finch] after he came to

CBS. They accepted me from the start, made me feel comfortable right away. So did Lance [Barrow] and that was important, obviously, because he was the boss."

Barrow retired from CBS at the end of 2020 after working for the network for forty-four years. He succeeded Chirkinian at the end of 1996 at almost the same time that CBS signed Feherty to his first contract after his three-tournament tryout.

Chirkinian was a diminutive man with a big voice. Barrow is a big man with a big voice, the classic barrel-chested Texan. He and Feherty hit it off right away, in part because Barrow realized that Feherty was a unique talent and had no desire to reel him in at all.

"Frank and Lance both deserve a lot of credit for hiring David," McCord says. "Even though he gave me a hard time that first day when I brought him to the booth at the International, Frank pulled me aside after we first hired him and said, 'McCord, that was a genius move you made with Feherty.' I've never forgotten that.

"But Lance was the boss when David started working full time, and saw what David brought to the table right away. It was his decision to put him on the ground and not in a tower, and that was a brilliant decision. The only person we had on the ground back then was Kostis, and his style was completely different than David's."

This was understandable. Kostis was a renowned swing coach whose greatest strength was breaking down players' swings on air. Feherty could certainly break down a swing if asked to, but his strength from day one was reacting to what he was seeing right in front of him and interacting with the other announcers, notably McCord.

"Gary and David together was a match made in heaven or a match made in hell, depending on your point of view," Barrow says.

"For me, it was heaven because they made our broadcasts different than anything else golf on television had ever seen or heard."

Soon after going to work for CBS, Feherty launched a writing career. It began with a column in a British golf magazine called *Golf Monthly*.

Feherty was well-known in Europe, for both his play and his humor, especially after his impromptu operatic performance of the popular ice cream commercial jingle following his first win, at the Italian Open. In today's world, the tape of that interview would be described as having gone viral. From that day forward, he was the golf pro who could have had a career singing opera.

"It was probably a bit over the top," David Jones says. "But he did belt it out that day."

Presumably, the magazine hired him for both his humor and his playing ability (if not his singing), but Feherty soon found that they were not enamored of his humor. "Put it this way," he says. "They didn't seem to be in love with the columns, and I certainly wasn't in love with the way I was being edited."

Enter *Golf Magazine*—based not in London but in New York—and editors George Peper, Jim Frank, and Mike Purkey. Their magazine couldn't possibly compete with the stable of players and former players that *Golf Digest* employed as "instruction editors."

The instruction sections have always been the key to the success of golf magazines. In those days, the covers of the glossy monthly magazines always had a headline that said something like, "Learn how Jack (Nicklaus) makes so many clutch putts" or "Tom Watson's secret to iron play." Those who played golf—and thus subscribed to or bought golf magazines—were convinced that the secret to becoming a better player was contained inside the pages of the golf magazines every month.

"When we did readership surveys, the ten most-read stories every month were instruction," Peper says. "After we hired David, he always came in eleventh."

Golf Digest liked to position itself as the game's "leading authority," and it built that claim around having big names on the staff—notably players, but also writers like Dan Jenkins, Dave Kindred, and Tom Callahan—men who had been writing well about the sport forever. When Jenkins talked (or wrote) about Ben Hogan, he did so from memory—having watched him play throughout most of his career.

Peper, who was *Golf*'s executive editor, and Frank, the managing editor, knew they couldn't compete with *Digest* for the biggest names in the game—although they did make a futile attempt to convince Woods's then-agent Hughes Norton to bring Woods to *Golf* as a "playing editor" when he emerged as a superstar in 1997. Pete McDaniel, who was Earl Woods's biographer, was on *Golf Digest*'s staff, so the chances that Tiger Woods would land with *Golf* were exactly zero. That didn't stop Norton from dragging out negotiations to get *Digest* to pay more and to try to manipulate Peper into—among other things—firing me because I wasn't writing about Woods in the same glowing terms (off the course) as the rest of the golf media.

"*Digest* sold itself as the game's authority," Peper says. "It circled its wagons around the icons of the game—people and events. We needed to circle their circle with some humor and with a more lighthearted approach than they took."

The person who pushed Peper and Frank hardest to hire Feherty was Purkey, who edited the noninstructional columns and features for the magazine. "Jim and I both liked him; we saw that he was a unique sort of talent," Peper says. "But it was Mike who pushed hardest for us to hire him."

Purkey had "discovered" Feherty during one of his first appearances as an announcer on television. After his two hours of fame in the booth with McCord during the summer of 1995, Feherty was hired by an independent syndicator to work the Johnnie Walker World Golf Championships, which in those days was a late-in-the-year "silly season" event in Jamaica.

"Loren Roberts hit a shot that was way left, went into a grove of coconut trees, rolled into the water, and somehow hit a floating coconut and popped out," Purkey remembers. "David was walking with the group. They went to a shot of David holding the coconut that Roberts's ball had hit. He held it up for the camera and said, 'I'm holding Loren Roberts's bruised nut.'

"After that, I started paying attention to what he was saying, and he was just flat-out funny. I thought if he could take that humor and put it into print, we'd have something. I wasn't sure he could do it because being funny in print is a lot harder than being funny live or on TV. But I thought it was absolutely worth a shot."

Peper and Frank liked the idea, especially because it meant bringing something to the magazine that they knew *Golf Digest* didn't have and almost certainly couldn't replicate.

Purkey assumed he would be ghostwriting the column the way he had done for Curtis Strange and for sports psychologist Dick Coop. "You don't expect a player or ex-player to be a writer," he says. "You expect them to give you some thoughts and ideas and then you put it together and present it to them in written form. When David's first column came in, I looked at it and was amazed. It needed almost no editing at all. He was a very good writer, *and* he was funny."

The only real challenge for Purkey was transcribing Feherty's handwritten words—which he faxed to Purkey—into a computer.

Later, he convinced Feherty to invest in a computer for his writing, which made his job much easier.

The two men became friends, and in 2002, when Feherty was working on his first book—*A Nasty Bit of Rough*—he called Purkey one day to tell him he was struggling with the writing. "I've got some chapters done and ideas for others, but I'm stalled," he said.

Purkey volunteered to fly down to Dallas to spend a couple of days helping out. When the book came out, Feherty sent Purkey a copy. The inscription said: "This is all your fault."

Purkey was touched.

Feherty was a star for *Golf* right away, the same way he had become a star for CBS right away. There was no way *Golf Digest* could find anyone who could come close to copying or duplicating Feherty, and even if Feherty had been interested in leaving *Golf,* there was no way the staid publishers of *Digest*—first the *New York Times,* later Conde Nast—were going to hire someone who wrote as far out of the box as Feherty.

The only person at *Golf Digest* who was allowed to write funny was Jenkins and that was only because he was Jenkins and because his humor was mild compared to Feherty's. Someone like Feherty—who wasn't a superstar back then—would never have been allowed to write the kinds of things for *Digest* that he wrote in *Golf* or said on CBS.

Part of Feherty's deal was to speak on occasion at outings for *Golf* and at corporate events for magazine sponsors. Once, Peper and Feherty were supposed to appear at an ESPN Zone in Chicago, one of the ESPN-run restaurants that mercifully disappeared in 2010. The ESPN Zones were seriously overpriced and the food was lousy—to put it kindly.

This was while they were still open, and it was also before the invention of GPS in cars. Feherty and Peper met at Chicago's O'Hare Airport, rented a car, and picked up a map.

"I knew Chicago a little; David didn't know it at all," Peper says. "I drove. David had the map. We were looking for the corner of Elm and Church—something like that. David's looking at the map's inset. He says, 'There's no fucking Elm Street.' I tell him to find Wacker because I know it's close to Wacker. He says, 'There's no fucking Wacker.' I *know* there's a fucking Wacker. I pull over and look at the map. It's a street map of Milwaukee."

Eventually, they somehow found the place.

When Peper talks about Feherty he brings up something Bernard Darwin once said of the English playwright, poet, and golfer Patric Dickinson. "Darwin said, 'Things occur to Patric that don't occur to the rest of us,'" Peper says. "That's David. Things occur to him that don't occur to the rest of us."

Golf put Feherty's column on the back page, and it was instantly popular with both readers and advertisers. "He did write a column once about Titleist, funny of course," Peper says. "Wally Uhlein [Titleist's CEO] was famously litigious and our lawyers were convinced we should kill the column. We didn't. Wally never sued, but Titleist was never a sponsor for any of David's columns."

Feherty always wrote fast, because he was more or less writing whatever was on his mind at that moment. He also rarely wrote long, a huge help to the magazine because a back page column can't jump. It has to fit onto the page. Feherty always did that.

Feherty went from being an injured, aging golfer looking for a place to play to a media star very quickly. The only week of the year he didn't enjoy working was the one many golf people look at as *the* week of the year: the Masters.

There is no event in golf that is treated with more reverence by the media—especially on TV—than the event played annually the second week in April in Augusta, Georgia. Some of the reverence is quite legitimate: the golf course, designed by Alister MacKenzie and Bobby Jones, is both scenic and wonderfully challenging for great players. MacKenzie also designed Cypress Point and Royal Melbourne, two other iconic courses, and Jones, who had won what was then golf's Grand Slam—US and British Opens, US and British Amateurs—in 1930, hired him to be the golf course's primary designer in 1930, soon after he retired from playing competitive golf at the age of twenty-eight. The two men worked together over the next several years on what became Augusta National Golf Club. Sadly, MacKenzie died in January 1934 at the age of sixty-four, a few months before the first Masters was played.

The Masters is unique among the four major championships. It is played at the same golf course every year and is the season's first major, a harbinger of spring to many in the United States. The golf course is aesthetically spectacular and uniquely challenging because its greens are so difficult. Because the membership is so wealthy, the grounds—golf course, clubhouse, practice areas—are always in pristine condition. You can literally toss a wrapper away and watch someone swoop in and pick it up before it hits the ground.

But the Masters is also uniquely reclusive and secretive. What's more, it has a pretty awful record when it comes to the treatment of minorities—all minorities.

No place in sports has more rules than Augusta National during Masters week. Try running to get to a good spot to watch, and you won't get three steps before security stops you. The club has its own language that TV partners are required to follow if they wish to remain TV partners. There aren't fans at Augusta National, only "patrons." And you certainly don't refer to a large number of patrons surrounding the eighteenth green as "a mob," as Jack Whitaker found out.

There's no front nine or back nine, just a "first nine" and a "second nine." There are no grandstands, just "patron viewing stands." There's no range, just a "tournament practice area." There is no rough; just a "first cut" and "second cut" where golf balls go when they don't find the fairway. Nothing at Augusta National is to be described as "rough."

There *are* "fairways" and "greens."

When I worked at Golf Channel, I was handed an eight-page list of Augusta National on-air dos and do nots. Among them were the fact that there was to be *no* reference to prize money—players ("participants," sorry) took part in the Masters for the honor of winning a green jacket, the tournament trophy, and a lifetime exemption to play in the Masters.

There was also to be no mention of the fact that Seve Ballesteros and Gary Player had failed to return their green jackets at the end of a year as champions, as is required. My first thought was, "How the hell would anyone even know that happened, unless the club told us?"

More important than all the silly rules inflicted annually on the golf, media, and spectator world is the club's troubling history with minorities. For many years, African American players who clearly should have been invited to play in the Masters were overlooked. It wasn't until 1974 when Lee Elder won the Monsanto Open soon after a rule had been passed that a victory on the PGA Tour had become a way to automatically qualify to play at Augusta that an African American got to play in the tournament; Elder was formally invited in 1975.

Forty-six years later, when Elder was eighty-six and dying, the club finally got around to asking him to take part as an honorary starter. Elder was so weak he could barely stand to wave to the crowd and couldn't walk onto the tee to join Jack Nicklaus and Gary Player in hitting opening tee shots.

If you read about Elder taking part in the opening ceremony or listened to what the TV "partners" had to say about it, you would have thought that Augusta National chairman Fred Ridley had authored the Emancipation Proclamation.

The club membership was all White until 1990, when the embarrassing debacle of Shoal Creek more or less forced it to invite a Black member. Shoal Creek was a club in Birmingham, Alabama, that was hosting the 1990 PGA Championship. When a reporter from the *Birmingham Post-Herald* asked club founder and president Hall Thompson what would happen if an African American applied for club membership, Thompson insisted that such a thing would never happen in Birmingham, adding, "We don't discriminate in any other area, except Blacks."

The ensuing uproar and the threat by many corporations to withdraw sponsorships almost led to the PGA being forced to move its championship to another golf club before a Black local insurance man, Louis J. Willie, was made an honorary club member. The PGA Tour then passed a rule saying that no club could host a PGA Tour event if it discriminated against anyone on the basis of race, creed, religion, or sex.

Technically, Augusta National was exempt from this rule since the Masters was not a PGA Tour–"sponsored" event, even though the Masters was—and is—part of the PGA Tour. Since Hall Thompson was a longtime Augusta National member, the club felt it had to do something in response to his embarrassing comment—

which he never apologized for. One month after the PGA Championship was played at Shoal Creek, Ron Townsend, a Gannett executive, became Augusta National's first Black member.

Hord Hardin, then the club's chairman, insisted he had been considering asking an African American to join the club before the Shoal Creek debacle, but very few people believed him. It took Augusta National another twenty-two years to ask a woman to join. In 2012, the club—which traditionally doesn't announce new members—very publicly announced that former secretary of state Condoleezza Rice and businesswoman Darla Moore had joined the club.

The club now has a handful of Black members and a smaller handful of female members. It is still very much a playground for rich White men, who make it clear to everyone who sets foot on their hallowed grounds that you play by their rules or you don't play at all. As Gary McCord found out.

Feherty had played in the Masters once—making the cut and finishing T-50 in 1992. He was paired for the first two rounds with Doug Ford, who had won the tournament in 1957 and was playing in his fortieth Masters that year. Ford would go on to play in nine more Masters—establishing a record broken in 2004 when Arnold Palmer played in his fiftieth—but he was almost seventy when he played with Feherty and had last made the cut in 1971.

He had once been a great player, winning two majors (the 1955 PGA in addition to the Masters), winning nineteen times on the PGA Tour, and playing on four Ryder Cup teams. He continued to play the Masters until 2001, hoping to become the first man to play in fifty Masters. But when he withdrew for a fourth straight year—after playing only nine holes—in his forty-ninth start, the Lords had seen enough. They informally passed what was known as "the Doug

Ford rule," sending letters to older past champions encouraging them to come and take part in pre-tournament festivities but not to play in the tournament, even though they had a "lifetime exemption" to tee it up on Thursday.

That was when Palmer and Nicklaus intervened on behalf of the past champions. Both denounced the rule, and Palmer went so far as to say he would stop playing the Masters after the 2002 tournament. When he was asked why he was going to stop playing, Palmer said with a smile on his face, "I don't want to get a letter."

Palmer hadn't made a cut since 1983, but he was never going to get a letter. Neither was Nicklaus. But past champions like Gay Brewer, Tommy Aaron, George Archer, and (strangely) three-time major champion and Hall of Famer Billy Casper, did get letters.

After Palmer threatened not to return, "the Doug Ford rule" was quietly rescinded. Ford, knowing when he wasn't wanted, never played in his fiftieth Masters. And so it was Palmer who was the first man to play fifty times. As usual, the Lords got their way. Nicklaus, for the record, played forty-five times—the last time in 2005 at the age of sixty-five.

Ford was finally elected to the World Golf Hall of Fame in 2011, his induction probably delayed by the infamy that "the Doug Ford Rule" brought him. He had been worthy of induction for a long time before finally being elected.

Ford did finish all thirty-six holes in 1992, and Feherty remembers enjoying playing with him. Feherty made the cut (+1) on the number and went on to finish tied for fiftieth place. Ironically, his fellow competitor from those first two rounds played in the Masters nine more times. Feherty never played in the tournament again.

The last year Ford played all thirty-six holes—1997—was the first year that Feherty worked the Masters as a broadcaster. More importantly, that was the year that Tiger Woods played the tournament for the first time as a professional—he'd played it twice as an amateur—and announced his arrival as a golf icon, winning the tournament by a stunning twelve shots.

Another Masters rule is that there are no TV announcers on the ground; no one is allowed to follow the players inside the ropes, as is permitted at other golf tournaments. As a result, Feherty was assigned to the fifteenth tower at Augusta. This was before the club had finally allowed CBS to show play on the "first nine," meaning Feherty's role was much more confined than when he would walk with the final pairing at other tournaments.

Jack Stephens, who was chairman of the club from 1991 to 1998, was always asked repeatedly in his annual Wednesday pre-tournament press conference about the club's refusal to allow CBS to cover the front nine the way the other majors allowed their TV partners to cover all eighteen holes.

Stephens was a believer that "the patrons" should have privileges TV viewers didn't have. One of those was access to the front ("first") nine.

One year, someone asked Stephens if he'd ever watched the Super Bowl.

Born and raised in Arkansas, Stephens had a deep southern accent that often caused people to underestimate his intellect. He wasn't a self-made billionaire oilman and investment banker by accident. Knowing exactly where the questioner was going, Stephens, without missing a beat, said, "The fourth quarter." That ended any pursuit of the "Why don't you allow TV to cover the front nine?" question for the day—and for the year.

"I just never felt completely comfortable there," Feherty says of his eighteen years as an announcer at Augusta. "I always worried I was going to say something that was going to get me in trouble and, as a result, get CBS in trouble. Obviously, I knew what had happened to Gary and I knew my sort of off-the-wall humor might not come off as funny to the membership. I was almost always nervous, and I was very careful about what I said."

Anyone who has ever done television from the Masters knows what Feherty is talking about. "They monitor everything you say very carefully," says Clampett, who worked Amen Corner for CBS from 1995 through 2006. "You always felt like you were working in handcuffs. My understanding was that a member was assigned to each individual announcer every day. I think we all appreciated the tournament for what it was, but the whole control thing was over the top."

I can speak firsthand to this. One year, while working for Golf Channel, I said on air that I felt badly for all "the people" who were being forced to leave the hallowed grounds during a lightning delay. I knew there was trouble when Rich Lerner, my on-air partner at that moment, used the word "patrons" about forty-seven times in the next two minutes. The second I was off air, I received a stern talking-to from my Golf Channel bosses. I probably deserved it. I knew exactly what I was doing when I said "people." If I had said I felt badly for the "mobs" being forced to leave, I almost certainly would have been fired on the spot.

Feherty learned about how seriously Augusta National took itself—and everything involved in the tournament—firsthand in 1998 when Ignacio Garrido hit three balls in the water at the fifteenth hole on Thursday and made an 11 on his way to a first-round 85.

"Well, most of the time you're happy if you have two ones on your scorecard," Feherty said as Garrido walked off the green.

The next day, then-chairman Jack Stephens took Feherty aside for a moment and brought up the comment. "We don't do cute at the Masters," he told him.

The fear that CBS announcers feel was never more evident than one Friday afternoon when Sean McDonough, who worked four Masters from the sixteenth tower in the early 1990s, realized he had mistakenly referred to the "patrons" as "fans" during first-round coverage the day before.

"Just wait until this afternoon," he said, sitting in the clubhouse before going on air. "There will be patrons all over the sixteenth hole. They will be behind the hole, next to the green, behind the green. They will be everywhere early and often. There will be patrons *swimming* in front of that green before I'm finished."

That may have actually been too cute (no bathing suits allowed at Augusta), but it sounded like a necessary walk-back. Anything to avoid the wrath of the men in the green jackets. No cute at the Masters, no fans (or people), and certainly no rough or a front nine or a back nine.

Feherty knew those stories long before his first Masters as an announcer. Plus, even though he spent a lot of time doing corporate speeches for very wealthy people, he was still the kid from Bangor who learned the game hanging out in the pro shop and sneaking onto the golf course and the driving range late in the day.

"It wasn't as if the people I met there weren't nice to me," he says. "They were. But I went into the clubhouse exactly once in the eighteen years I did the tournament and that was when someone invited me to lunch. I just never felt as if I was as good sitting on that tower, feeling the way I did, as I was at other tournaments."

One person who doesn't agree with Feherty on his performance is Barrow, his old boss.

"I know David always felt that way," he says. "He always thought maybe he didn't belong on a tower at Augusta. But I really think that was just in his mind, because I thought he was terrific at the Masters. He wasn't doing the same job as he usually did week to week and that made him feel a little bit uncomfortable. But if you go back and listen to the telecasts, he was wonderful.

"I still remember in '03 when Mike Weir was trying to come from behind on the last day and he hit a critical shot to the fifteenth green, David just said, 'Oh, Canada!' It was perfect. He was almost never off key and his humor was always there."

Tommy Roy, who became Feherty's boss at NBC, says that one of the reasons he wanted to hire Feherty was his work at Augusta. "He had exactly the right tone, I thought," he says. "He was respectful of the event and the traditions but never went over the top with it."

Dan Hicks agrees. "I know being in a tower and being at Augusta was different for him, and I can understand why he felt as if he didn't really fit in there," he says. "But I honestly thought some of his best CBS moments were during the Masters. The majors *are* different. You need a different tone; you need to understand what's at stake. I honestly thought David was terrific at the Masters, although I know he never loved it there."

The days at Augusta were long ones for Feherty. He had to be in the tower early in the day to prepare to go on in the early afternoon. When CBS went off the air, Feherty was supposed to ride a cart into Butler Cabin and tape the Thursday–Friday late-night show with Nantz once all play for the day was complete. Right from the beginning, Barrow wanted Feherty to be Nantz's partner on the late-night shows, in part because of his ability to analyze but also to bring a bit of levity to the oh-so-serious place.

Feherty never drank before or during a live telecast, but he did occasionally drink during the break between the live telecast and the taped late-night telecast, if only to kill time with nothing to do.

One night, after he'd had a few drinks, he drove his cart from the tower at fifteen to Butler Cabin and went to move his car from the CBS lot to a spot next to Butler Cabin in order to make a quick escape once the taping was over.

"That was my first mistake," he says.

His second was getting lost in the dark—it is very dark in that area of the club at night—and missing the small parking area next to Butler Cabin by a wide margin. Instead, he drove around Butler Cabin and found himself on the nine-hole, par-3 golf course that becomes the center of the golf world on Wednesday of Masters week during the par-3 tournament.

There was no golf being played at that moment, and Feherty realized quickly he was someplace he should not be.

"So, I turned the car around and drove back around the cabin," he says. "As soon as I got there, I saw two police cars."

Feherty waited in the car for one of the police officers to come to talk to him. "When he first walked up, I saw on his uniform that his name was O'Reilly. Irish. I thought, 'Maybe there's a chance I can get out of this.'"

He never gave himself a chance to find out if being Irish would help because Officer O'Reilly opened the conversation by saying, "Sir, have you been drinking?" At that moment, Feherty's sixth-sense Irish humor took over, which was unfortunate.

"Well, officer," Feherty answered, "if that's your first question, I know why you didn't make detective."

A moment later he was in zip-tie handcuffs. A potential disaster seemed likely. Since they were on the grounds of Augusta National, the police put in a call to Stephens, who was still the club's chairman at that point.

The police told Stephens what had happened and asked him what he wanted done with Feherty.

According to what Feherty was told later, Stephens thought a moment and then said, "Just let him go." Maybe Stephens knew that Feherty had become friends with his son, Warren. Maybe Stephens, who had a sneaky sense of humor, appreciated Feherty's sense of humor. Or maybe Stephens, like so many others, just liked Feherty enough to give him a mulligan.

The police let Feherty go, and he did the late-night show without missing a beat.

He also never drank again on the grounds of Augusta National. Exactly why Stephens chose to let Feherty go that night will never be known for certain since he passed away in 2005.

Stephens was a graduate of the Naval Academy—the football field inside Navy–Marine Corps Stadium is named for him because he gave so much money to the school. He was also something of a legend at Augusta National for finding humor in most situations.

One story told about him—which people who have worked there swear is true—is about the day another member showed up with a guest, who wondered on the first tee what the stakes of the day's match would be.

"Five thousand a hole?" he asked. "Ten thousand a hole? What'll it be?"

"Around here," Stephens replied in his Arkansas drawl, "we usually like to play a dollar Nassau."

His point was simple: no need to show people how rich we are by playing for high stakes.

The guest apparently grumbled all day about playing for such low stakes and was still grumbling when the group went inside for lunch.

Finally, Stephens had apparently heard enough.

"How much are you worth?" he asked.

Proudly, the guest replied, "Forty-two million dollars."

Stephens nodded, turned to a waiter and asked for a deck of cards. Placing the deck on the table he said, "Forty-two million dollars? How about I cut you for it?"

The guest never said another word. And the member who had invited him was told in no uncertain terms not to *ever* invite him back.

Feherty could appreciate a sense of humor like that. "For a billionaire," he likes to say, "Jack was a pretty damn good guy."

David practicing in his favorite footwear.

David with his first mentor, David Jones.

David in a familiar spot at the '82 Irish Open.
He still won.

David with the Dunhill Cup trophy he clinched with brilliant 4-iron at the Road Hole.

Opening ceremony "The War by the Shore."

David and Anita with the Outstanding Civilian Service Award.

With confidant Tom Watson.

David in 2022.

David and Shey—a
joyful father and son.

The Feherty family. Shey is on the far right.

The Fehertys today: Erin, Rory, David, and Anita.

Billy and Vi's kids: Helen, David, and Deborah.

Billy and Vi's kids a few years later.

Helen, David, and Deborah with their dad.

Anita, Erin, David, Deborah, Vi, and Helen.

David and Shey.

David and Rory.

At St. Andrews in 1990.
He was in the top ten until the
back nine on Sunday.

David and Anita at David's third LIV event in Chicago.

Vi, David, Erin, and
Deborah, Christmas 2022.

CHAPTER SEVEN

One Step Forward ...

Tom Watson's intervention on Prince Edward Island in July 2006 was a turning point in David Feherty's battle with alcoholism. Sadly, it was an interlude, not an ending.

Watson's AA group in Kansas City directed Feherty to a group in Dallas that they thought would work for him. "It was a clean air group," Feherty says. "No smoking during meetings. That actually mattered to me. It helped."

For a while, the meetings worked. Feherty got up most mornings when he was home, got on his bicycle, and rode to a meeting. Then, one morning, he got up, got on the bicycle, and just kept riding without stopping at the AA meeting.

"He called me from somewhere north of McKinney, which is about thirty-five miles north of our house," Anita Feherty remembers. "He said he hadn't gone to the meeting, but he had worn himself out riding and was ready to come home and take a nap. I went and picked him up."

After that morning, Feherty's "meeting" became a lengthy bike ride each day. Initially, it worked well—very well. He would ride until he was tired, stop for coffee somewhere, and then go home.

"Riding the bike became my meetings," he says. "I got to be quite good, I could go fifty miles easily. It wore my body out, but I'd feel mentally refreshed. It was almost like a form of meditation, although I was always very careful about what I was doing."

He was being careful on a February morning in 2008 and was almost home when he was slammed into from behind by a pickup truck. "I was on Park Lane, approaching the light at Bed, Bath & Beyond when a pickup truck knocked me into the Beyond section," he wrote, months later, in *D* magazine, a glossy Dallas magazine with a largely upscale subscriber list.

As it turned out the trailer section of the truck—wider than the truck itself—was what struck Feherty. It sent him flying off the bike. "My head snapped back and I began to fly, like a silhouette of E.T. across the moon," he wrote in the same magazine piece.

He didn't know it at that moment, but he had a collapsed lung, three broken ribs, a separated left shoulder, and a crushed left elbow. He was also bleeding profusely from various cuts suffered when he landed.

A woman he didn't know came instantly to his aid and—apparently—called for an ambulance. Feherty remembers hearing the driver, who was never charged with anything, saying, "He shouldn't have been in the road."

That comment, which he was in no position to respond to at that moment since he couldn't speak, was especially galling to Feherty, who always wore *two* red lights to make sure he could be seen: one on his helmet and one on the back of his riding jersey.

"Looking back, I'm a little surprised and I suppose I should be grateful he stopped at all," he says. "I guess he wanted to be sure he hadn't killed me."

Feherty's recovery took months and several surgeries. He managed to make it to the Masters six weeks after the accident, but ended up back in the hospital needing more surgery after he returned home. It was, to put it mildly, a nightmare.

The accident changed a lot of things in his life—none of them good. Feherty had been sober for almost two years, and the bike had become his addiction and his daily AA meeting. Most days he was up and on the bike before sunrise and home for breakfast with Anita shortly after sunrise.

He was turning fifty that summer and, even though he was now very much a star at CBS, the thought of playing in at least a handful of Senior PGA Tour events had crossed his mind. He undoubtedly would not have had to go to Q-school since he was exactly the kind of "name" senior events loved and would have gotten a sponsor's exemption to play whenever he asked for one.

"Looking back, I probably would *not* have tried the Senior Tour," he says. "At that point I hadn't tried to play competitively for a dozen years. It may have crossed my mind, which is why I wrote it [in the *D* magazine piece], but I'm pretty certain I wouldn't have done it. I think I was just angry that the guy who hit me took the option away—even if I ultimately had decided not to take it."

The crushed elbow took away any thought of playing competitively again because it made it impossible for him to play at all. Feherty had dealt with elbow issues during his career on the European Tour. He often says, "My addiction to painkillers was the result of pain in my elbows, and the pain from my first marriage."

As it turned out, Feherty didn't play another round of golf for fourteen years. Two more serious bicycle accidents, neither as damaging as the first one but still serious, ended any thoughts about playing the Senior Tour at all, not to mention any thoughts about playing in outings or just for fun. The third accident—which occurred in 2015—ended his time as a regular bike rider, other than short rides near home.

"I had all sorts of minor accidents too," he says, able to laugh at some of the memories years later. "I was on a ride in West Virginia near the Greenbrier when I saw a black bear on the road. A moment later, her two cubs followed her, and I had to swerve severely to avoid hitting one of them while going pretty fast. Another time I was attacked by a flock of turkeys. I lost control of the bike once when I saw a snake in the road and landed in the emergency room again. There was also a coot that came out of the water one time and dove at the pedals. It was wiped out, but so was I. I swear it seemed for a while as if the entire animal kingdom was out to get me."

He smiles. "After a while, my credit card was on file at the emergency room near our house. I think they kept an open tab there for me."

After the third serious accident—the second one had also come in 2008—he had to give up any serious riding completely.

"Just couldn't do it anymore," he says. "I had too many things wrong with my body to keep riding for anything more than a few minutes near home. That was a real loss for me."

There was one funny bicycle moment before he had to give up riding for good. In 2013, he was taping a *Feherty* interview with Paul Azinger. For an interview with Tom Watson earlier that year, he had ridden a horse since Watson had become enamored of horses because of his wife Hilary's love of horse-cutting. Watson had learned to horse-cut and, even after Hilary's death in November 2019, he continued to take part in horse-cutting competitions.

"Hilary was a scratch as a horse-cutter," Watson says. "I was more like a 10-handicap. But I got better at it."

When he decided he could no longer play competitive golf, Watson continued to horse-cut. "It's something I can still try and get better at," he says. "I love to compete, and this is a way I can compete."

Feherty was nowhere close to a 10-handicap horseman. "Put it this way," Watson says. "David on a horse when we did the show was not a pretty sight. But he was willing to give it a shot."

Feherty was almost always game to give something a shot if a guest enjoyed doing it. Azinger wanted Feherty to watch him ride his motorcycle. Feherty wasn't getting on a motorcycle, but he agreed to follow Azinger on a bike, both men miked up so they could talk. It wasn't an especially brilliant idea from the start. While Azinger got on his motorcycle, Feherty got on a bicycle, wearing a helmet that Azinger had supplied. Azinger zoomed off, and Feherty followed. It was hopeless, of course. He can be heard saying, "I can't see very well with this helmet on," just before he crashed into a bank of bushes, not one hundred yards from his starting spot.

It took Feherty a while to untangle and get up, but he was uninjured. The camera crew kept rolling even as Feherty struggled to get off the bike and out of the bushes, and it made for a hilarious two-minute segment of the show. When Azinger watched the tape with Feherty, he couldn't stop laughing. In the end, it was a classic *Feherty* moment.

The accidents on the road, especially the first one, were no laughing matter. Feherty had finally found what seemed like the perfect way to stay sober: no rehab, no meetings, perhaps most important, no *people*. He became fascinated with bikes, building them from scratch when he wasn't riding them. At the time of the first accident, he had six different bikes that he took turns riding.

"He needed something to distract him from the idea of drinking, from his dark moments, and the bike had become exactly that," Anita says. "It was perfect for him. Was he addicted to bicycles? Sure. Addicts need something, and David's an addict. This was a lot better than alcohol or drugs by a wide margin."

It was also good for his overall health. His weight, after reaching as much as 245 pounds once upon a time, came down steadily. He was a healthy five-foot-eleven and 175 pounds. He wasn't crazy skinny the way he had been when Anita first met him in 1995, and he wasn't fat either.

"I actually felt as good as I had felt in years and years," he says. "I was enjoying my work and my family. I still had plenty of issues, I'll always have those. But until the bike accident I was probably doing as well as I had done since I left home at seventeen to turn pro."

Unable to ride his bike and still feeling the aftereffects of the accident, he became depressed. He had always had depression issues, but they had never been diagnosed. Getting out of bed in the morning became difficult. He had constant aches and pains that should not have lingered for as long as they had or been as serious as they continued to be. He went to his primary care doctor, who, after examining him, told him he needed to see a psychiatrist because there was nothing he could find that was physically wrong that should cause the kinds of pain he was in.

Naturally, finding the right psychiatrist was a challenge. "First guy asked me if I drank," he says. "I said I used to drink a lot, but right now I'm not drinking. It turned out *he* was an alcoholic."

Four doctors later, Feherty finally found a psychiatrist he trusted, Dr. Art Arauzo. He still sees Dr. Arauzo regularly, fourteen years after starting with him.

More than anything, Feherty needed more work. Being at home for too long, especially after the bike accident, made him restless. Anita was still working, the boys were growing up, and Erin was in school every day. That left a lot of alone time for Feherty.

Not good.

"Never good for me to be alone with nothing to do," he says. "Boredom isn't good for me, and it isn't good for me just to lie around by myself. I actually like to travel because it keeps my mind busy."

Anita agrees: "He needs to be busy. If he has nothing to do, he goes to dark places," she says. "His mind needs to be occupied, and he needs to have something to prepare for, to focus on. He probably needs less time to prepare than 99 percent of the people in the world, but it's still good for him to have something specific he's looking forward to doing and getting ready to do. It doesn't matter if it is TV, speaking, or being on stage. As terrified as he gets before performing, he loves it. He needs it."

It wasn't as if he didn't have a lot to do: he had his full CBS schedule, which usually consisted of twenty events a year. He had also become an in-demand corporate speaker, which added a good deal of income and some extra travel to his schedule. Still, he needed more.

Enter Dick Ebersol, who had been running NBC Sports since 1989. Comcast, which owned Golf Channel, had bought NBC-Universal for $30 billion late in 2009. Golf Channel was soon rebranded with NBC logos and Ebersol, a huge golf fan, showed up in their Florida studios not long after the FCC had approved the sale. Soon afterward, he installed Mike McCarley, who had been his public relations person for twelve years, as the new Golf Channel president.

"Dick was the one who really wanted to bring David into the fold in some way, shape, or form," Elkin says. "Mike [McCarley] played a major role and so did Tom Stathakes and Keith Allo. But it all started with Dick wanting David working for NBC in some way, shape, or form."

That way, shape, and form, after some false starts, eventually became *Feherty*.

Ebersol recognized that Feherty was a unique talent, and he left it to McCarley; Stathakes, who was the vice president for programming at the time; and Keith Allo, the network's lead features producer, to put the show together.

This came after a proposed situation comedy—called *F*, starring Feherty as himself—had been shot and then abandoned before the pilot even aired because it was so bad. It was Stathakes, then vice president for programming at Golf Channel, who made the decision not to air the pilot.

"We wanted David working for us," Stathakes says. "He was exactly the kind of talent that we needed at Golf Channel because he wasn't just another ex-player talking about how wonderful every single shot he saw was or why a bad shot wasn't really the player's fault.

"I certainly wanted to have guys who appreciated how hard the game can be working for us, but we needed an injection of humor on our air. We needed people who didn't see golf as deadly serious. David had the potential to bring that—we all knew that.

"But the sitcom just didn't work. It looked good, it was professionally done, but it had one basic problem: it wasn't funny. I sent it to Ebersol, knowing how badly he wanted David working in some form for NBC. He agreed with me, and so did Keith. We decided we should try something else."

That decision turned out to be critically important for Feherty and for Golf Channel. A new idea was hatched that called for Feherty to host a show in which he would interview golf's biggest names. At first, the show was going to be thirty minutes. But that was quickly changed to sixty minutes.

"Once you put the commercials into the show you had, at most, twenty-two minutes," Feherty says. "If you were going to do the interviews right, you needed more time than that."

Feherty was still under contract to CBS, but his contract allowed him to do the show even though Golf Channel was an NBC property. Once, the thought of someone employed by one network working for another network in any form would have been considered impossible. But with all the multiple platforms owned by different networks, it is now commonplace. Since *Feherty* was completely different from the work Feherty was doing for CBS, the network was willing to allow Feherty to branch out.

The first show aired on June 20, 2011—the day after Rory McIlroy had won the US Open at Congressional Country Club. Ten weeks earlier, McIlroy had his first up-close encounter with the David Feherty whom people love so much.

He had led the Masters by four shots after fifty-four holes and looked as if he would become a Masters champion a month before his twenty-second birthday. But it all crashed on Sunday. He shot 80 and tumbled to a tie for fifteenth place. Afterward, he handled himself with remarkable grace, answering every single question asked by the media and saying—among other things—"If this is the worst thing that ever happens to me, it'll mean I've had a pretty good life."

Feherty saw that interview but was still concerned about McIlroy. He had first met him in 2009, when McIlroy came to play in the United States and their backgrounds and temperaments made them instant friends.

"I mean, we grew up five miles apart," McIlroy says. "Different generations of course. I first really knew of him when he started working for CBS and I would stay up at night to watch the tournaments being telecast in Holywood on Saturdays and Sundays.

"I knew he'd been a good player, but as a kid, I don't think I knew how good. I just thought he was very smart and very funny on air."

When McIlroy came from behind in May 2010 on the last day of what was known then as the Quail Hollow Championship, it was Feherty who walked the last few holes with him for CBS. McIlroy ended up shooting 62 to win by four shots, holing a fifty-foot putt on eighteen to put an exclamation mark on his win.

"It was cool to have David walking with us on the back nine," he remembers. "And then he did the post-round interview and I could tell how excited and happy he was for me. I always felt that, quietly, he was always looking out for me. He never reached out to me when he needed something, only when he thought I needed something."

That was what happened on the last day of the 2011 Masters. As soon as he got off the air, Feherty contacted Chubby Chandler, who was then McIlroy's agent, to find out where McIlroy was staying. "I didn't want to call because it wouldn't be the same, and he would say, 'I'm OK, thanks for calling,'" Feherty says. "I got the address from Chubby and just drove to the house."

The house was right near the golf club. Feherty found McIlroy and several of his boyhood mates, who had come over for the week, playing soccer on the front lawn.

"We all went inside and sat down around a round table and David started to talk," McIlroy says. "For the next hour, maybe longer, he did what kind of became his stand-up act. At one point, I was laughing so hard—we all were—that I was almost crying. I remember thinking, 'This is the second time I've cried today, but this time feels a lot better.' It was just classic David. He was going to be *sure* I didn't spend the night sulking and being sad."

Afterward, Feherty made sure to get a minute alone with McIlroy to be 100 percent certain he was all right. "The kid really was OK," he says. "I was amazed at how mature he was. Then he went out and *proved* he was OK two months later."

He proved it by winning the US Open at Congressional Country Club by *eight* shots. When Gerry McIlroy greeted his son coming off the eighteenth green after his victory, McIlroy said simply, "Happy Father's Day."

Indeed.

The next night, *Feherty* debuted. The guest was Lee Trevino, Feherty's boyhood hero.

Most European players of Feherty's generation will tell you their first golf hero was Jack Nicklaus, who was the world's dominant player during Feherty's formative years as a player. But it was Trevino whom Feherty looked up to the most.

"It was a lot of things," he says. "Some of it, certainly, was his back story: poor Mexican kid who grew up in Texas with nothing and made himself into a great player. A lot of it was his sense of humor: he took golf seriously but never took himself seriously. And he was a truly great player. He was the reason I developed my swing so I would hit the ball left to right. No one hit it left to right better than Trevino."

Trevino's father left home when he was very young and he was raised by his mother and his grandfather—who was a gravedigger.

He left school at the age of fourteen to work as a caddie and to pound golf balls in his free time. At seventeen, he joined the marines and spent four years as an enlisted man—not the typical résumé for a future Hall-of-Fame golfer.

He turned pro when he came back from the marines and—like Feherty—started out as a club pro. By 1967, he had finished fifth in the US Open, and a year later, at the age of twenty-eight (Trevino is fifty-two days older than Nicklaus), he won the Open and became a sudden star, in part because he was a great player, in part because of his unique personality.

He always seemed comfortable under pressure. "Pressure isn't a putt that's the difference between first and second," he once said. "Pressure is a putt for ten dollars when you've got nothing in your pocket."

He was comfortable with fans and with the media. The one place he wasn't comfortable was Augusta National Golf Club.

It was his left-to-right ball flight that always made the Masters Trevino's Achilles' heel. He won the other three majors twice each but never finished higher than T-10 (twice) in twenty Masters appearances. He made it clear almost from the beginning that he wasn't comfortable at Augusta National and skipped the tournament in 1970 and 1971 even though, as a major champion, he was invited. When he returned in 1972, he changed his shoes out of the trunk of his car and told people he wasn't comfortable with the club's membership. He was quick to point out that if he wasn't a major champion, the only way he'd be allowed on the club grounds was through the kitchen.

Years later, Trevino softened on the club. In 1989, at the age of forty-nine, he was the oldest man to hold the first-round lead in the

Masters after shooting a 5-under-par 67. He finished T-18 that year, his seventh top-twenty finish at Augusta. By comparison he had eight top tens at the US Open, seven at the British Open, and six at the PGA. He won the PGA, the last of his six major titles, in 1984 at the age of forty-three.

"No offense to anyone else, but I wanted Lee to be my first guest," Feherty says. "I knew he'd be great, but it was much more personal than that. If we had never done another show after that one, I'd have thought the whole thing was worthwhile."

Rather than having the production staff reach out to Trevino, Feherty drove to Preston Trail Golf Club—which is outside Dallas—knowing that was where Trevino hung out most of the time. He found Trevino in the clubhouse and explained he was launching a new show and that he very much wanted Trevino to be the first guest.

"I'd love to do it," Trevino said.

Feherty ended up doing 150 shows during a ten-year span, and even though every big name in golf—except for Tiger Woods— appeared on the show, he went well beyond golf for his guests. Four presidents—Bill Clinton, George W. Bush, Barack Obama, and (cough, cough) Donald Trump—were interviewed by Feherty. Obama was part of a pre-Olympics show on NBC. Feherty's politics are somewhere between Obama and Trump, closest perhaps to Bush among the presidents who appeared on the show, but all play golf and all were willing to sit down with Feherty.

The show was expensive to produce because it often involved traveling to the interviewee's home, a lot of preproduction work, and a research staff who helped make Feherty into a very good interviewer.

"It was a lot more than that," says Allo, who was the show's executive producer from episode 1 to episode 150. "David has a way of making people feel comfortable, even if there are a bunch of cameras in the room."

The show was a hit from the start—in part because of the big names who willingly sat to be interviewed by Feherty, but at least as much because Feherty's interviewing style was unique and because the show was completely different from anything anyone had seen on Golf Channel in the past.

"He was great at making you feel comfortable," Watson says. "You felt like you were having a conversation with a friend more than you felt like you were being interviewed, even though there were cameras all over the place."

The interviews were thoroughly researched by Feherty and his staff, but perhaps more important, Feherty had a knack for making guests, even guests who had been interviewed hundreds of times, feel comfortable.

"I think his style was disarming," says Elkin, who admits he's biased. "The people he interviewed knew he'd always been open about the issues in his life, that he had no secrets. And, he has that self-deprecating manner that makes people feel comfortable."

Feherty even got Bob Knight, who had become something of a recluse after retiring from coaching in 2008, to come on the show. "We lured him by telling him he could come and fish in Kyle Bass's lake," Feherty says, laughing. "We had [Feherty's Troops First Foundation] events at Kyle's place quite often, and we told Knight he could fish in Kyle's lake if he did the show. Knight LOVES to fish. He came up and we did the show there. He was great."

Feherty actually got Knight to show him how to throw a chair during the show, a perfect example of his ability to get people to talk about moments in their lives that most interviewers wouldn't dare bring up.

That was in 2013, and Feherty was busy all the time. He was working for CBS, doing *Feherty*, doing about thirty speeches a year (going rate roughly $65,000 per appearance), and had established Feherty's Troops First Foundation.

The genesis of Troops First was a trip to Iraq that Feherty made in 2007 under the auspices of the USO. There were two groups that went to visit American troops that spring: a number of big-name college basketball coaches and a group of golfers and golf people that included Feherty, Tom Watson, Butch Harmon, Tom Lehman, Donnie Hammond, and Golf Channel's Kelly Tilghman. The basketball coaches included Michigan State's Tom Izzo, Notre Dame's Mike Brey, and Maryland's Gary Williams.

"I grew up in an urban war zone," Feherty says. "But what I saw over there and what those guys were dealing with was at another level. I went over there an Irishman and came back an American. I wanted to find ways to help these guys—not just when they were over there but when they came home."

Feherty vividly remembers the moment when he knew he wanted to do more. The golf group was being flown in a C-130 back to Baghdad for their flight home. Quite suddenly, the plane made a U-turn in midair, which, in the middle of a war zone, was both baffling and frightening. When the group asked what had led to the sudden turn, the answer came back quickly: "We have to make an HR stop."

"No one knew quite what to think for a moment," Feherty says. "Our first thought, of course, was what the hell did human resources have to do with this? Then, when the guy we'd asked realized we didn't understand, he said, 'An HR stop means we're stopping to pick up human remains.'"

When the plane landed, a flag-draped coffin was rolled on board. Inside was the body of an army ranger who had been killed in action. The coffin traveled with the group, first to Baghdad and then to Ramstein Air Force Base in Germany. "To say that it was sobering is a vast understatement," Feherty says.

There was a lighter moment when the group got to Germany— for everyone but Lehman. Feherty had loaned him two different types of sleeping pills to help him get through the flight from Baghdad to Ramstein. The pills worked so well that Lehman was still groggy when they landed and was having trouble walking. When a customs official asked what was wrong with him, Feherty answered, "Oh, it's no big deal; it's just the drugs."

Before he could explain that the drugs were sleeping pills, Lehman was marched away to be questioned and apparently spent a day being interrogated before it was decided he'd just taken a couple of sleeping pills and nothing more.

"Lucky for me they didn't check my luggage closely," Feherty says. "I might still be there."

Feherty travels at all times with a small pharmacy of drugs. He takes thirteen different pills on most days. Among them are Vraylar, which is for bipolar disorder; Cymbalta, which is an antidepression medication; and Lamictal, which is a mood stabilizer. "I don't understand that one," he says. "If you are in a crappy mood why would you want to stabilize *that*?"

Feherty describes Vraylar as a "turbo-charged antidepressant." He also takes a staggering amount of Adderall, which helps with his ADD, and Vyvanse, which also helps with hyperactivity. "The Adderall would keep a racehorse awake," he says, laughing. Feherty has been prescribed a lot of what he calls "psyche meds," plus Atorvastin for hypertension and Ambien and Remeron to help him sleep.

"The Remeron is like a little velvet sledgehammer," he says, while admitting there are still nights when he struggles with insomnia.

His sleeping issues were so well-known at CBS that Lance Barrow had a small couch in his office that Feherty often slept on before telecasts.

"When we knew he was in there sleeping, we all tiptoed around and talked in whispers," Jim Nantz says, laughing. "His need to sleep was genuine and our need to have him alert and ready when it was time to go on air was just as genuine."

Barrow remembers Feherty as being low maintenance—except for his need to sleep in his office. "So, we'd have our production meetings someplace else," he says. "It was no big deal. And he really didn't need to be in the production meetings. If there was something unusual he needed to know about, I told him about it when he woke up."

Feherty carries his various pills around in bottles stuffed with one of each that he takes daily. It is, to put it mildly, an essential part of his travel gear.

In 2019, when the British Open was played at Portrush in Northern Ireland, his pills somehow got lost on the trip across the Atlantic. "I knew there was no way I could make it through the week without them," he says. "I mean, no way. They couldn't have put me on the air."

Hicks, who was sharing a house there with Feherty, Roger Maltbie, and Jimmy Roberts, vividly remembers the two days Feherty was briefly without his meds: "He was completely miserable," he says. "All he could do was lie on the couch. If he moved at all, it was obvious he was in terrible pain. Thank goodness Anita figured out a way to get the drugs through customs and to him before we were supposed to go on the air."

David called Anita at home, and she was able to put together enough pills to get him through the week; then she got all sorts of doctors' notes in order to get the pills through customs and had someone fly to New York with the pills. There, they were handed to an NBC technician who was flying to London and then to Belfast. He was able to get the pills to Feherty.

"I was two days without them, and I was really hurting," he says. "I either lost them going through customs or someone stole them. Not really sure which. But if I had any doubts at all about needing the meds, they went away during those two days."

Feherty came home from that first trip to Iraq absolutely determined to do more to help those who were in the military or had served in the military. He got in touch with Rick Kell, who had been one of the organizers of the trip to Iraq, and said, "I think we can do more to entertain those guys than we did on that USO trip."

Kell agreed, and Feherty's Troops First Foundation was born. Initially, it involved getting more people to make the trip to Iraq. Eventually, Feherty and Kell realized that those coming home also needed help assimilating back into society and moving on with their lives, so the two men began working with the Wounded Warriors Project, to put on events for soldiers and ex-soldiers after they returned from war.

"President [George W.] Bush's Iraq war was not a popular war in this country," Feherty says. "Guys coming home weren't treated as heroes the way those coming home from some other wars were and the way, more often than not, they're treated today. It's very hard for anyone to understand how difficult it is, whether you've been wounded or not, to come back. They all suffer wounds. It's just that some of them can't be seen."

Troops First now sponsors numerous events each year, all to raise money but also to give those who have fought overseas days they can enjoy. The group has worked with Wounded Warriors on different events, including golf tournaments, bird-hunting trips, and fishing contests. Among other things, Troops First raised enough money to build seven "transition" homes for men and women coming out of lengthy stays at Walter Reed Hospital in Bethesda, Maryland.

"It gives them a chance to catch their breath while they figure out where they're going to go next and what they're going to do with their lives," Feherty says. "They're nice houses in a nice location, and we don't rush anyone in or out."

Feherty began the process of becoming an American citizen soon after his 2007 return from Iraq. On February 23, 2010, he was sworn in with about forty others as an American citizen during a ceremony at DFW Airport in Dallas–Fort Worth. Among those who flew in for the ceremony was Tom Watson.

"It was a very emotional day," Watson says. "You could see how much it meant to David and to the others who were taking the oath. What was most remarkable were the number of men and women who had been touched by Troops First, who came out to show support for David. It was really something to see."

One of the many ex-soldiers who came to Troops First events was Chris Kyle, who had become known as the "American Sniper" after his 2012 autobiography that recounts in detail his exploits while in Iraq. Kyle, who served in the navy from 1999 to 2009, claimed 160 "kills" with his sniper rifle. The navy never confirmed that number, but there is no doubt he shot a lot of people. In 2013, Clint Eastwood directed a movie based on Kyle's life that came out shortly after Kyle and a friend had been murdered at a shooting range by another veteran who was apparently suffering from a serious case of PTSD.

Feherty had become fascinated with guns after his bicycle accidents. One of the people he met at one of his events was a young man named John Wayne Walding. Born in Waco, Texas (on the Fourth of July), Walding had been a Green Beret sniper in Iraq and had lost a leg. He was getting ready to go to community college when he met Feherty.

"Kid was a badass," Feherty remembers. "I thought he should do something badass, not go to community college. I suggested he learn how to *make* sniper guns that people could use for hunting. We went to a gun store in Dallas that was run by a guy called Dick Cook, who was one of the founders of the Gunsmith Association of America. He took us to his lathe and showed us how to make a sniper rifle.

"I ended up buying a lathe and putting it in my garage, and we started a company called Five Toes Custom Gunworks—because John had five toes. It's been very successful."

Feherty still makes sniper rifles—but only the kind that can shoot one shot at a time. He gives most of them away. Feherty rarely hunts himself. "Every once in a while when a feral pig gets on to my property, I will shoot them because if I don't, they'll destroy the whole place," he says. "Occasionally, I will go bird hunting as part of one of our events.

"Generally speaking, I'm not comfortable hunting animals. I like to shoot targets. That's become my AA meeting—going to shoot targets."

Feherty now owns a farm outside Dallas and has a target range there. But his favorite spot is a range just over the Texas-Oklahoma line where he can shoot as far as a mile. It is about eighty minutes from his home, and he frequently drives out there for the day with an ex-military friend or two so he has someone to shoot with during the day.

"Addicts need something to be addicted to," he says. "I've gone from alcohol and drugs to bicycles to guns. I know how dangerous they can be if you don't know what you're doing. Fortunately, I do know what I'm doing."

It was Kyle who actually taught Feherty how to shoot a sniper rifle. Like Bob Knight, he came to an event at Kyle Bass's farm and, while there, showed Feherty how to shoot one.

"He literally laid down on top of me," Feherty remembers. "He taught me how to listen to my heart beating—it wasn't that hard to hear with him on top of me—and the gun in my hands. He told me, 'Shoot in between heartbeats.' It took a while, but I got the hang of it. Now, I'm pretty good at it."

Fortunately for Feherty, his wife has no problem with his addiction to shooting or guns. Anita grew up in Mississippi and is a pretty good shot herself. She doesn't often go on David's shooting trips, but she is fine with him going—especially as long as he's only shooting targets.

"I enjoy skeet shooting and target shooting, and I'm fine with shotguns," she says. "Rifles don't thrill me. They're loud, and I honestly don't like being around them. I'd prefer David stick to shotguns, but if going off to shoot keeps him between the yellow lines of life, I can deal with it."

The trips to the target range don't always thrill Anita. "He has a lot of friends who watch out for him, who keep him between those yellow lines," she says. "But it isn't true of all of them. Some are enablers. I worry about them. I have to worry. I work my butt off to try to protect him from himself. It isn't an easy job."

Anita Feherty laughs when people point out to her that she's been a very patient woman for twenty-seven years. "No kidding," she says. "No kidding."

CHAPTER EIGHT

Stardom

Between his work for CBS, *Feherty*, his speaking engagements, and his work with Troops First, Feherty kept very busy after he renewed his contract with CBS in 2009.

By then, he had a new television agent, Andy Elkin, who worked for CAA, having moved to Los Angeles without a job after practicing law briefly in New York. "I practiced law for two years," Elkin says. "Which was long enough to know I didn't want to practice law."

Feherty had written four books in the aughts—three collections of his *Golf Magazine* columns, the other a uniquely Feherty-esque work of fiction. A man named Webb Stone had been involved in the publication of the books and, as a result, had some idea about Feherty's TV contracts.

"He thought David should be doing better," Elkin says. "He contacted me and asked if I was interested in talking to him."

Elkin had played golf all his life. In fact, his father had moved his family from Brooklyn to central New Jersey in order to have access to affordable public golf courses. He was also a golf fan and had become very familiar by then with Feherty's work on CBS. He called David and Anita and asked if he could fly to Dallas and meet with them.

"I liked him because he was almost an un-agent," Feherty says. "Obviously, part of what he thought he could do was make me more money. But he talked a lot more about work I could be doing that went beyond calling tournaments on television."

In fact, it was Elkin who first went to CBS to explore the possibility of getting Feherty involved in programming that went beyond his tournament schedule. There was even talk about creating an Andy Rooney–like segment for him on *60 Minutes*.

Feherty's wit would have been perfect for the role. Exactly where his politics would have fit in is hard to know. "I'd have been interested to give it a try," he says. "But I don't think the news people ever thought it was a very good idea."

He actually filmed a test segment for the role. According to a magazine story written by Franz Lidz for *Golf World*, the topic was the three times it is permissible to laugh at a funeral. According to Feherty, one was if you didn't like the deceased, two was if the casket got dropped, and three—Feherty told Lidz he couldn't remember.

CBS never made him an offer.

Soon after that, NBC Sports president Dick Ebersol and Golf Channel came into the picture with the idea of Feherty doing something that didn't involve golf tournaments. When CBS couldn't come up with a non-tournament outlet for Feherty, NBC was able to do so because it owned Golf Channel. Of course, CBS owned both Showtime and the CBS Sports Network, but the programming on those networks is so remarkably dull that Feherty never would have fit in. His show would have been much too smart for either one.

With Elkin doing the negotiating, Feherty re-upped with CBS in 2009 for another five years. Fortunately, the contract was constructed in such a way that Feherty had the ability to work for another network as long as he wasn't actually calling golf for anyone other than CBS. That was how the first *Feherty* contract for Golf Channel got done.

"I really think Dick wanted to eventually have David be all in at NBC," Elkin says. "I felt like that was in the back of his mind right from the beginning."

As successful as *Feherty* quickly became, he still managed to find troublesome moments in his professional life. Feherty had written the lengthy piece for *D* magazine after his bicycle accident in 2008. The piece had been both funny and biting and, as Mike Purkey and the readers of *Golf Magazine* could attest, was well written. A year later, Feherty was one of several people asked to write about former president George W. Bush's impending move to a Dallas suburb.

Feherty was a fan of Bush's and gladly took on the assignment.

As usual, Feherty was all over the map, giving various reasons why Bush wouldn't like his new neighborhood. But he also ventured outside the initial premise of the piece and wrote the following paragraph: "From my own experiences visiting the Middle East, I can tell you this though: despite how the conflict was portrayed by our glorious media, if you gave any U.S. soldier a gun with two bullets in it and he found himself in an elevator with Nancy Pelosi, Harry Reid, and Osama Bin Laden, there's a good chance that Nancy Pelosi would get shot twice and Harry Reid and Bin Laden would be strangled to death."

Pelosi was Speaker of the House of Representatives and Reid was the Senate majority leader—the two leading Democrats in Congress.

The piece was published in May 2009 and, needless to say, sparked seriously angry backlash against Feherty.

CBS quickly issued a statement condemning what Feherty had written: "While outside his work for CBS, David Feherty is a popular humorist, we want to be clear that this column for a Dallas magazine is an unacceptable attempt at humor and is not in any way endorsed, condemned, or approved by CBS Sports."

The statement came from LeslieAnne Wade, who was CBS's vice president for public relations at the time. That it was Wade who put out the statement was clear proof that CBS was trying to downplay the impact of the comments as much as possible—pointing out that CBS was *not* involved in the magazine piece and keeping CBS Sports president Sean McManus and Lance Barrow, Feherty's boss, above the fray. A statement from McManus would have made clear what everyone knew: CBS was freaking out.

"They had a canary," Feherty says, years later. "I was under strict orders from LeslieAnne and [CBS's primary golf PR person] Robin Brendle to not say a word to anyone. I was allowed to speak two words if the subject ever came up: 'no comment.'"

Wade's statement was straight from the Sergeant Schultz "I know nothing" handbook—condemning Feherty's comments without condemning Feherty and making it clear that CBS, to paraphrase the iconic *Hogan's Heroes* character Sergeant Schultz, "knew nothing."

Feherty issued his own apology in a statement carefully edited by Wade and Brendle: "This passage was a metaphor to describe how American troops felt about our 43d President [Bush]," the statement said. "In retrospect, it was inappropriate and unacceptable and has clearly insulted Speaker Pelosi and Senator Reid, and, for that, I apologize. As for our troops, they know I will continue to do as much as I can for them both at home and abroad."

Even today, Feherty looks back on the incident with regret. "Was I in any way trying to say that the Speaker of the House and the Senate majority leader should be attacked—killed?" he asks. "No. I was saying that troops serving in Iraq were probably not their biggest fans, but I phrased it in a way that clearly came out wrong.

"I've always tended to push the envelope a lot—especially back then. I also wrote in that column that I believe in the death penalty, especially for pro-lifers, child molesters, those opposed to gay marriage, and for stupid dancing in the end zone. A lot of that was over the line too, but in a different way, in a way people could read it and know I was going for funny.

"Talking about the possibility of anyone killing the Speaker of the House and the Senate majority leader clearly wasn't funny."

It's entirely possible that in today's world, Feherty wouldn't have survived those comments. "Honestly, I don't think I would have, not today," he says. "The world has changed a lot since then. I think the chances are, if I said something close to that today, CBS—or NBC—probably would have had to fire me."

The case can be made that most people would have been fired for comments like that, even in 2009. Ben Wright had been fired by CBS in 1995 for saying that lesbians were hurting the popularity of women's golf and that women had difficulty swinging a golf club because their "boobs" got in the way. As tasteless and foolish as those comments were, they didn't imply that it would somehow be OK to murder the Speaker of the House of Representatives and the Senate majority leader.

In fact, on his then nightly show *Countdown*, MSNBC's Keith Olbermann attributed the comments to "soon to be ex-CBS Sports golf analyst David Feherty."

Olbermann had it wrong. Feherty wasn't fired. In fact, he survived—and thrived—because he was Feherty; because golf fans loved him, because CBS knew it, and because people understood the comment wasn't so much malicious as a (badly) botched attempt at humor.

"You go outside the box often enough, you're going to crash and burn on occasion," Feherty says. "In the end I was lucky I didn't burn. The CBS people were like a wall protecting me after it happened."

Sometimes in life, mea culpa is enough. Especially if you're David Feherty.

Feherty having lived to tell about his political gaffe, his career continued to grow.

Feherty came about after the failed attempt at a sitcom in which Feherty was to play himself and find himself in various outrageous situations. The pilot called for him to cover the Westminster Dog Show with well-known comedian Fred Willard in a featured role.

Fortunately, for all involved, Tom Stathakes recognized that it wasn't very good right away.

Stathakes had been hired by Comcast—which had bought Golf Channel in 2003—to try to improve the overall quality of the channel. Golf Channel had acquired the first- and second-round rights to PGA Tour events in 2007, and Stathakes's marching orders were direct: make Golf Channel better. In those days, it was little more than an on-air public relations arm for the PGA Tour and all things golf. Ironically, after Stathakes left and Mike McCarley took over as Golf Channel's president, it reverted to what it had been prior to Stathakes's arrival.

After killing the sitcom, Stathakes and his top people came up with the idea to make Feherty an interviewer, not an interviewee, to have someone irreverent asking questions as opposed to people who treated golfers as if they were godlike figures. In fact, Stathakes specifically said back then, "We need people working here who don't think Jesus Christ plays on the PGA Tour."

"David had become a big name in golf by then," he says. "Getting him at all would be a coup, and my sense was he wanted to do something different. But it wouldn't do us any good to make a big deal out of getting him and then put on a show that wasn't any good."

Stathakes, Golf Channel president Page Thompson, and Allo flew to Dallas to meet with David and Anita. There, they presented the idea for *Feherty*. Both were intrigued and turned him over to Elkin to negotiate a deal.

Elkin, having been unable to convince CBS to do anything with Feherty that went beyond working tournaments, loved the idea of adding something new to his client's CV.

A few months later, Feherty and Elkin met with Stathakes and Allo in a hotel room in Los Angeles. "I handed him a contract that was for five years and $4 million," Stathakes says.

And so, *Feherty* was launched.

"I knew it was going to work," Stathakes says. "We were prepared to put a lot of money into producing it, but more important, we had David. There just wasn't anyone out there like him. It wasn't as if we could say, 'OK, we didn't get Feherty, who do we go after now?' It had to be Feherty. I knew he would be able to get great guests. But I don't think I ever dreamed that truly famous people *not* in golf would be clamoring to come on."

Stathakes actually introduced Feherty to the Golf Channel staff in a theater setting, a two-hundred-seat theater in the Florida Mall, which was not far from the Golf Channel offices in Orlando. He and Thompson talked to the group—which, for the most part, had no clue what was going on—about expanding Golf Channel's reach, about coming up with new and different programming. That had been Stathakes's mandate when he'd been hired. Finally, after a good deal of metaphoric drumrolls, Stathakes introduced Feherty, who walked in from the back of the room to wild applause.

"We all knew this was a breakthrough," says NBC's Courtney Holt, who would play a major role in booking guests and handling logistics for the show. "There was no way this was going to be just another Golf Channel–type show. We all knew it. This was a big deal."

Feherty took Feherty to a new level of fame—and fortune— because, even though it was on Golf Channel, non-golf fans frequently watched since many of the guests weren't golfers. It made him the rarest of people in sports: someone who transcended his sport in terms of celebrity. The list of sports *announcers* who have done that through the years is as follows: Howard Cosell. John Madden. And Feherty.

"What was great, is that, after a while, truly famous and important people *wanted* to be on the show," Keith Allo says. "And David never took anything for granted. He worked just as hard on the Shane Lowry interview in 2020 as he did on the Lee Trevino interview in 2011. He wanted every show to be high quality."

Lowry, the 2019 British Open champion, was the final guest on *Feherty*.

Trump was easily the most eager presidential guest—appearing twice, once before he was president and once after being elected. He owns a number of golf courses and wanted desperately to host a men's major championship at one of his properties. His course in Bedminster, New Jersey, hosted the women's US Open in 2017 and was scheduled to host the men's PGA Championship in 2022 until the attempted insurrection at the Capitol building on January 6, 2021.

Four days after the attempted insurrection, the PGA of America announced it would move the event to a different golf course. Trump—surprise—was furious. He was already feuding with the PGA Tour because it had moved its World Golf Championship event from Trump-owned Doral in Miami to Mexico in 2017. Doral had hosted a PGA Tour event every year from 1962 to 2016, but when Trump's presence made it difficult—impossible?—for the tour to find a new title sponsor after Cadillac left in 2016, Doral, which by then was known as Trump-Doral, was abandoned.

When Rory McIlroy heard the news about the tour leaving Doral for Mexico he quipped, "Well, I guess we'll all just have to jump over that wall," referring to the wall Trump was proposing to build—and eventually built—along the US-Mexico border.

Feherty says nice things about all the presidents he interviewed, and while his politics are probably closer to Bush's than to the other three, it's clear his favorite was Clinton.

"I remember he walked in and said to me, 'I always wanted to meet you because I know you're as full of it as I am,'" he says, doing his very good imitation of Clinton.

Clinton was a fan of Feherty's before he was asked to be on the show. "I had watched it and loved it," he says. "David has a way of getting people to answer difficult questions without making them sound difficult. I think a lot of it has to do with the fact that he doesn't take himself seriously."

Clinton says when he was asked to do the show, "I jumped at the chance. I said right away that I'd like to do it."

The show was taped in a hotel suite in Tampa. Clinton was in town for a speech and the interview was scheduled for that day. Feherty's first question was direct: "Why in the world would you do this?"

Clinton laughed, shrugged, and said, "Because I like the show."

"I thought he did a great job with the interview, and when I watched the show [after it had been edited for time], I was happy with the way it came out," Clinton says. "I was having some trouble with my voice because I'd had some stomach issues and was on some meds, but other than that, I was very happy with the way it came across. I enjoyed the whole experience."

Feherty not only interviewed Bush 43 but also interviewed Condoleezza Rice, Bush's secretary of state and one of Augusta National's first two female members.

The Obama interview was much shorter than a *Feherty* interview, but Feherty did get him to talk about his handicap, which had pretty much been a state secret during his years as president. Obama "revealed" his handicap to Feherty, saying, contrary to reports that he was a 17, he was actually a 13.

Most successful TV shows are copied: every shouting-match show on ESPN is a not-very-good copy of Tony Kornheiser and Michael Wilbon's *Pardon the Interruption*. But no one attempted to copy *Feherty* because there's no one like Feherty, and even people working in television understood that.

"David was like a secret weapon," Allo says. "No matter what anyone else tried to do, no matter what kind of guests they might get, none of them had David."

In the end, among the many mistakes Golf Channel made when it began to bleed money—in large part because it vastly overpaid the PGA Tour to extend its rights to televise tournaments—none was worse than canceling *Feherty*.

The given excuse was that the pandemic made it impossible to travel to the homes of potential interviewees. That was certainly true, but the show could have been put on hiatus until the pandemic was over. Instead, with no warning, it was canceled after an interview with 2019 British Open champion Shane Lowry that aired in August 2020.

"I was told it wasn't the pandemic, that the decision had been made before it started," Feherty says. "I never had a chance to say goodbye to all the people I'd worked with on the show for almost ten years. It really was hugely disappointing."

Anita Feherty goes further than "disappointing": "It was heartbreaking," she says. "He had worked for ten years with this great crew. They had become friends. It would have been one thing if they had given us some warning, 'Hey, this is the last show,' or even that they were thinking of canceling the show, but there was nothing. The way they did it was almost cruel—for everyone."

CHAPTER NINE

Another Stage

EVEN BEFORE *FEHERTY* WAS LAUNCHED, Feherty had been in great demand as a speaker. He did corporate outings, usually for an asking price of about $65,000 per speech, and he did charity events for friends all the time. He also spoke at Troops First events, usually at dinner after the day was done.

He probably could have gotten paid more at the golf outings where he spoke if he still played golf, but he couldn't. Instead of playing, he would ride around in a golf cart, finding ways to insult the players—especially the celebrities—in each group. He was one of those rare speakers who was often invited back because he always seemed to have fresh material.

Barry Terjeson was still handling his speaking, even after Andy Elkin had taken over his TV deals. It was Terjeson who got the call early in 2014 from a Canadian concert promoter named Brad Jones.

Jones was forty and had grown up in London, Ontario. He had first been exposed to Feherty in 2004, when Mike Weir—who had won the Masters in 2003, becoming the first Canadian and the first left-handed player to win at Augusta—and hockey player Dino

Ciccarelli came to London to do a fundraiser. Comedian George Lopez was also there, and so was Wayne Gretzky, hockey's Great One. A number of Canadian musicians performed. So did Feherty.

"He was great," Jones remembers. "Had everyone cracking up. The audience loved him. A bunch of my friends were there and they loved him. Everyone did."

Feherty's memory of that trip has strictly to do with Gretzky. "We had no problem getting into Canada back then just showing our driver's licenses. But the US required a passport to get back in if you weren't a citizen—which I wasn't. When they told me that—remember this isn't all that long after 9/11—I honestly thought, 'I'm never getting out of Canada.'

"That's where Wayne came in. He said, 'Don't worry, we'll get you out.' Four of us drove to the border and when we got there, the guard took one look at Wayne and went completely crazy. Wayne started talking to him and when he went on about how his father was Wayne's biggest fan, Wayne said, 'Let's give him a call.' So, they called the father. In the meantime, we handed over three passports and one driver's license. All came right back stamped for entry.

"Wayne hung up with the dad, we waved to the guard, and we crossed into the US. I turned to Wayne and said, 'You really *are* the Great One.'"

Feherty had only been on stage for a few minutes during that '04 event, but Jones remembered him. Ten years later, a local children's hospital in London asked Jones if he could book James Taylor for their annual fundraiser. He had no luck with Taylor. That was when several of his friends, remembering 2004, suggested he try to get Feherty. Different act than James Taylor certainly, but undoubtedly a lot funnier.

Jones called Golf Channel and was directed to Terjeson, who, having gotten his price, booked the date. That was the first time that Jones and Feherty actually met.

"We'd bought a bunch of books [*A Nasty Bit of Rough*] to give to our biggest donors," Jones says. "I called him and asked if I could bring the books over to his hotel. He came to the door wearing boxer shorts and a white T-shirt with a mustard stain on it. We sat and talked while I handed him books and he signed them.

"That night he performed in front of 1,600 people and knocked it out of the park. When he came offstage, they're still standing and cheering, so I sent him back out. Then, when he came back, I said to him, 'Have you ever thought about doing stand-up?'

"He said, 'Isn't that what I just did?'

"I laughed and told him I had an idea. The next day, before he left, I handed him an Excel spreadsheet showing him how much I thought could be made if he did stand-up on a regular basis in front of audiences like the one he'd performed for the night before."

Jones laughs. "I could tell he wasn't really paying attention, but he stuck what I gave him in his jacket pocket."

And completely forgot about it. "I really wasn't even listening to what Brad was saying that morning," Feherty says. "I didn't give it another thought."

A day later, Jones got a call from Anita Feherty. She had found his spreadsheet in David's jacket pocket and wanted him to explain it to her.

"She liked the idea," Jones says. "I think she knew right away he'd be good at it—especially since I said he didn't need to do anything different than what he'd done at our fundraiser. I told her that if my spreadsheet was close to being right, he'd make twice the money he was already making from corporate speeches."

Anita was certainly intrigued by the money. But beyond that, she liked the idea of her husband having more to do. "Busier the better," she says. "Plus, I knew Jonesy was right, that he'd be good at it."

The Fehertys agreed to a two-night tryout that summer: one night in Edmonton and one night in Calgary. Jones chartered a luxurious plane—a Citation CJ2—to get Feherty from Edmonton to Calgary after the first night. "I wanted to make him feel like a big-time celebrity," Jones says. "I thought that would make it more enjoyable for him."

Since he didn't have a real advertising budget, Jones had flyers made up and paid someone in each town to drive to every local golf club and hand out the flyers. "We had one hall that seated 1,800 and another that seated 1,700," Jones says. "We sold them both out. People knew who David Feherty was, and they were willing to pay to hear his act."

The only problem the first night was getting Feherty offstage. Once he got started, he couldn't stop.

"I was petrified with fear before I went out there," he says. "I knew I was just doing what I'd done in the past, but it *was* different. People were paying *just* to see me. There was no dinner or charity cause they were also paying for. That was scary.

"Of course, the other part of it was that I'm *always* petrified when I go on stage or I'm performing in any context. I'm always convinced my ADD is going to kick in, and I'm going to lose my place and freeze out there."

He didn't freeze at all. In fact, he stayed on stage for more than three hours as one story led to another story, which led to another story.

"The last hour I was doing jumping-jacks backstage to try and get his attention and get him off," Jones says. "By the time he stopped, he was completely exhausted. But, my God, they loved him."

The next night, Jones convinced Feherty to stop after two hours—still much longer than almost any stand-up comic ever does in a set, but a time Feherty was comfortable with from that day forward.

On the way to the airport after the second night, Jones handed Feherty an oversized check he'd had made. It was for a million dollars. It also wasn't real.

"He asked me if he could cash it at an ATM," Jones remembers, laughing. "I told him no—but that I was trying to make the point to him that I could make him at least that much the next year if we put together a schedule and he was willing to travel," Jones says. "If nothing else, it got his attention."

The whole weekend got Feherty's attention. He enjoyed the "celebrity" treatment—"I really couldn't believe it," he says of the plane, the way the audiences reacted to him, and Jones's notion that he could continue to do this and make a lot of money. Plus, adding to his travel schedule was more a plus than a minus because, as Anita pointed out, he always does better when he's busy. What's more, if he could travel privately, Anita could come with him—a huge bonus for both of them.

And so, *Feherty Off Tour* was born. The plan was eight weeks a year, three nights each week. Often, he would do three cities in three nights—traveling by charter plane in between.

"It just would have been too exhausting if I'd had to deal with a commercial flight three mornings in a row," he says. "The private planes had to be part of the deal—for me and for Anita."

The money coming in made that possible. Early on, Jones tried to schedule Feherty in cities where the PGA Tour was going to be.

When the PGA Tour comes to most towns, it is *the* sports story that week. Having a celebrity with a connection to the tour was a natural for selling tickets. Feherty played small towns and big ones. His performances were almost always sold out. He eventually pared the act down to an hour and forty minutes of stand-up, followed by twenty minutes of Q&A. That was still a remarkably long time for a stand-up comic to perform and Feherty never worked with a script. Even so, he always left the audience wanting more.

As word of mouth about the act spread, so did locales. By the time the pandemic hit, Feherty had performed in more than one hundred cities, including places like Indianapolis, Detroit, Cincinnati, Atlanta, Charleston, and Richmond. He once played three straight nights in Naples, Florida, and sold out a 1,700-seat theater all three nights.

Jones declared him to be "the Celine Dion of Naples," referencing his fellow Canadian, who also happens to be a golf fan and a golfer.

Feherty has also played plenty of small towns, including Wilkes-Barre, Pennsylvania, where he opened the show by saying he assumed the town was named after John Wilkes Booth. Again, edgy humor he can somehow get away with that others wouldn't dare think about trying.

Right from the start, Jones found another way to monetize the act by adding a meet-and-greet aspect to the evening. From the beginning, tickets were priced between fifty-nine and sixty-nine dollars, depending on the venue. But, for an extra one hundred dollars, a ticket buyer could arrive early, get to meet Feherty, and have a brief chat with him. Each got a signed book and an autographed picture, and Feherty would warm himself up by telling the VIPs a few stories that would not be part of the act when the rest of the audience was let into the theater. There were a total of 150 VIP passes for sale, and invariably, they sold out.

Feherty's act is basically his life story. He talks about growing up during the Troubles and about his family—his mom, dad, and two sisters. He talks about his drinking and about Caroline. Some of the things he says about Caroline are right on the line between funny and mean. Feherty doesn't mind if some people think he goes over the line on occasion.

He tells hilarious stories about Rodney Wooler (a.k.a. Mucker), his late caddie from his European Tour days who made Feherty look like he'd never had a drink in his life if you compared the two men. He talks about Tiger's greatness and tells the pilot joke.

"There are lots of others," he will tell his audience. "But that's the best one." Most of the others are too dirty to repeat in polite company.

The only subject off-limits for his humor is his family. He works with a desk behind him that is a mock-up of the desk he worked from on *Feherty*. Often, Anita travels with him, and he will introduce her at the end of his act. If she's not there, he settles for a photo of her that sits on the desk—his only prop. There's the desk, the photo of Anita, and a stuffed chicken named "Frank," first made famous as a prop on *Feherty*.

If you were to attend one of the shows as a VIP and spend a few minutes talking to Feherty and then listening to him talk to the smaller audience, you would think he was having the time of his life for the twenty minutes he spends with the group of 150 before he goes backstage to rest for a few minutes while the rest of the audience is coming in and finding seats.

The truth is, Feherty would much prefer spending that pre-performance time alone in the green room freaking out about what is to come. But he not only does the VIP mingle before every performance but also charms everyone he meets. Imagine, 150 new best friends at every show.

Dan Hicks, his former NBC colleague, says he would introduce Feherty to an audience this way: "Meet the funniest, most genuine, good-hearted soul you'll ever meet. And when this is over, you'll have a friend for life."

That's exactly the way the audience feels when Feherty finishes.

He has the ability to do that whenever he is in public, no matter how uncomfortable he might feel. Anita, Rory, and Erin all tell stories about spotting people in airports or restaurants who clearly want to come up to Feherty but hesitate, perhaps because they're shy, perhaps because they don't want to interrupt him.

"Sometimes, I'll just point at someone and say, 'Go say hello to him or her," Anita says. "He always does it, and you can just see the person light up that David Feherty would actually come over to talk to *them*. I know he'd be perfectly happy if that never happened, but he never says no. He goes and does it."

"That's the great thing about him," Jones says. "He has a true knack for making everyone feel important."

Perhaps that's because he's never felt as if *he* was important.

CHAPTER TEN

Steps Backward

THE DRINKING STARTED AGAIN IN the summer of 2016. David Feherty was at a friend's farm outside Dallas. He was alone when he spotted the bottle of whiskey.

"It was as if it was speaking to me," he says. "It was saying, 'Come to me. I'm here for you.' I've always had an incredible capacity for Bushmills. Unfortunately, I listened to what the bottle was saying to me."

Feherty knows now—knew then—that as an alcoholic he couldn't just have one drink or drink once. As soon as he opened the whiskey, all the memories about *why* he liked to drink came flooding back the way they always had in the past.

He had to fly to Rio de Janeiro in early August to work the Olympics for NBC. Keith Allo went with him so he would have company during the hours he wasn't working.

"The good news," Allo remembers, "was that they kept him very busy. He wasn't just working at the golf course. They had him on one show after another because they knew he could add to the telecasts. It wasn't as if the golf was a major priority for them. Getting David on air was."

The problem was they were staying at a hotel that was close enough to the athletes' village that security made coming and going difficult. Most nights, when he was finished working, Feherty had dinner at the hotel with Allo. Then they went to bed.

At least Allo did.

"I didn't realize it at the time, but there was a rooftop bar in the hotel, and he was going up there by himself and drinking. He's often told me that when he drinks it's because he's trying to slow his mind down, to shut it down if he can. He's like Brick in *Cat on a Hot Tin Roof*. He drinks until he hears the click."

Unfortunately, after so many years of drinking, it can take a while to feel the click.

Feherty's work at the Olympics was unaffected. He's been a functioning alcoholic for so many years that he can drink at night and be ready to work in the morning.

When he went home, Anita discovered him with a bottle of vodka in the garage. Not surprisingly, she flipped out. "First thing I did was call Tom [Watson]," she says. "By then, that was what I did when I felt I needed help with him. Tom said, 'I'll be right there.'"

Watson got on a private plane and flew from Kansas City to Dallas. It was time, they decided, for an intervention. "We felt like we had no choice," Anita says. "David needed professional help. We didn't think he was likely to just stop drinking on his own at that point in his life."

Anita and Watson brought five other people with them that day: Dr. David Genecov was the Fehertys' next-door neighbor; Rick Kell had worked closely with Feherty from the start on Troops First; Ed Garahan had also worked for Troops First; Donny Durbin was a former marine who owned a local gun store; and John Wayne Walding was Feherty's partner in the sniper gun–making company.

They all said the same thing to Feherty that people say at interventions: "We love you and you need help. Let us help you."

And as often happens at interventions, the subject was furious.

"I was pissed off then, and to be honest, I'm still pissed off about it now," he says. "They were insisting that I needed to go to rehab. I didn't want to go, and I knew rehab wasn't the right thing for me. It never had been. I had been able to get sober in the past without rehab, and I was convinced I could get sober again without it. What really upset me was that none of them knew I was drinking again until the intervention. Why were they brought in then, but never in the past?"

The group was insistent. "They weren't leaving until I agreed to go," he says. "It wasn't as if they said, 'Let's discuss this.' It had already been discussed. My opinion didn't matter. I felt trapped."

Watson had already made arrangements through a friend to get him into rehab at the Mayo Clinic in Minnesota. It had been a doctor at the clinic who had recommended Art Arauzo, Feherty's psychiatrist, to him eight years earlier. For that, Feherty was grateful. Arauzo's presence in his life—which continues to this day because of that recommendation from the Mayo Clinic—was a major reason he grudgingly got on the plane.

Feherty finally agreed to go with Watson, even though he still hated the idea of rehab. As both he and Anita have explained, he's not good in groups when he's not in control—a dynamic arguably essential to rehab.

Feherty and Watson flew to Rochester, Minnesota, on September 6. Feherty was evaluated and the doctors recommended he enter a twenty-eight-day rehab program that began two days later. He lasted ten days.

"It might have been the worst experience of my life," he says. "The thing is, I was good at drinking. No one ever knew except Anita, and I'd always found a way to stop. Rehab was terrible. The first two days they had me in the psych ward, and they strapped me to a table. Did I need *that*? No."

Then came the coloring book.

"They gave me a coloring book for adults and told me to read it and color in it. What the hell is a coloring book for adults? The answer's simple: it's a coloring book! Every day I thought the same thing: What am I doing here? Finally, I just left. I think if I had stayed any longer, I might have died. That's how much I hated being there."

He left without checking out, went to the airport, and had four drinks while waiting for his plane. So much for getting sober.

"I was angry about it then; I'm angry about it now," he says. "It never should have happened. An intervention like that should only happen if everyone believes the only way for someone to get sober is rehab. If nothing else, I had proven in the past that I could get sober without rehab."

If David hasn't gotten over the experience, neither has Anita.

"The last thing he did willingly was get on the plane with Tom, and he wasn't very happy about that either," she says. "From the moment he checked in, he was fighting the whole thing. It was as if he was trying to prove he was right, that he shouldn't be there.

"The people at the clinic told me later that he never said a word in any of the sessions. He made it clear to everyone he didn't want to be there. Then he left without even checking himself out. Just left. They told me they didn't see much point in trying to get him to come back because they could only help people who were willing to be helped. David wasn't willing. He was going to prove that we were all wrong to send him there in the first place. His goal when he went there wasn't to get sober, it was to prove the intervention was the wrong thing for us to do."

A week after returning from the clinic, Feherty flew back to Minnesota—this time to work the Ryder Cup for NBC outside Minneapolis. He told a handful of people what had happened and that he was afraid every night that he was going to drink again. One night, his friend and Golf Channel colleague Kelly Tilghman sat up with him until dawn to keep him distracted so he wouldn't be tempted to drink.

In the six years since, Anita Feherty has never held another intervention, and she has never tried to get her husband to go back to rehab. "I work my butt off to try to help him stay sober," she says. "I love him dearly, that's why I'm still here. But it's not easy. It's never easy."

In the aftermath of the failed trip to rehab, Feherty became more aware than ever that he wasn't the only member of his family with an addiction issue.

Shey had turned twenty-eight on July 29, 2016—shortly before his father went into rehab.

He had left his job working in a restaurant to start a ticket resale business, and it wasn't going very well. He'd had issues with drugs in the past, notably cocaine. Now, he was using the drug again.

Everyone in the family knew the person Shey went to for money when he needed to buy drugs was his father. "Dad could never say no to Shey," Rory Feherty remembers. "I'm sure some of it was feeling guilty about being an absent father and the issues between him and our mom. But it was more than that. Shey could manipulate people. He was charming, and he could lie with an absolutely straight face easily. If there was one thing he was always very good at, it was manipulating people. And there was no one he manipulated more than Dad."

David Feherty doesn't dispute that on any level. "The truth is, I couldn't resist the kid. It wasn't just that I loved him as his dad, but he seemed so innocent—even in his twenties—about things. Honestly, he was the sweetest boy you'd ever meet. He'd ask me for money and swear it wasn't for drugs, and I believed him. I believed him because I *wanted* to believe him. I knew he was lying. I was lying too—to myself.

"It got to the point where I was told quite pointedly that I had to stay away from him, that I had to stop giving him money. I didn't mean to be, but I was his number one enabler."

Shey was living with his mother at that point, which no one thought was a great idea. "It was kind of a continuation of what our life had been for a long time, hearing from both sides how wrong the other one was all the time," Rory says. "It couldn't have been healthy. It *wasn't* healthy. It never was.

"I think there were times when we were young and even after we were grown-ups that we both felt caught completely in the middle. The storylines we got from each of our parents on who was the bad guy were so radically different. It was easier to handle when we got older because we just accepted it being that way, but it had to leave scars from when we were younger."

On the Fourth of July in 2017, Anita got a text from Shey saying he thought he needed to go back to rehab. When something practical needed to be done, the boys turned to Anita.

"When we were young, I thought of Anita as being very stern," Rory says. "My mom was the lax one, and Dad wasn't there a lot of the time. It was only when I got older that I realized Anita wasn't so much stern as the person who took care of us. All five kids. And Dad."

Anita told Shey she would be glad to help and to let her know when he was ready and wanted her to start the ball rolling. She never heard back.

On July 28, David and Anita agreed it would be OK to call Shey the next day to wish him a happy birthday. David hadn't spoken to his son for several months.

Rory, who was getting ready to deploy in a few months to Djibouti as part of his commitment to the National Guard, worked a late night/early morning stint on the twenty-eighth and twenty-ninth at the Denton County Sheriff's office, where he is now a sergeant. He had made a note to call his brother for his birthday and tell him he would see him in a few days and was looking for a birthday present for him.

"I got home from work at about 2:30 in the morning," he says. "Before I went to bed, I called Shey and left him a birthday message. It was short; I said, 'Happy birthday. I love you. See you soon.' I figured that way he'd have it when he woke up in the morning. Then, I went to sleep."

A few hours later, Rory woke up much earlier than usual, at about seven o'clock. "Normally when I have a shift that starts at two o'clock, which I had that day, I wake up about eleven thirty or twelve," he says. "For some reason, I woke up early that morning. I have no idea why. I turned on my phone, and it was blowing up with messages."

The messages were from his mother, who was in a state of panic. She had found Shey in the bathroom with blood coming from his mouth and had called 911. She had kept trying to text Rory, until she left one final message, apparently after the paramedics arrived: "He's dead, Ror."

"That was it, those three words," Rory says. "All I remember saying when I read that message was, 'Aah shit.' There was a sense of disbelief. I mean my brother was dead. But there was also a feeling that we all knew there was a strong possibility it would come to this. His whole life was a struggle."

Rory got in his car to drive to his mother's house in Plano, hoping he would get to see his brother. He was on the Lewisville Bridge, driving from Denton to Plano, when he reached Anita.

"I just told her that Shey was dead," he says. "There wasn't very much more I could say. I really didn't know much else at that point. My mom was too hysterical to tell me anything. Anita said, 'You need to tell your dad.'"

It was at that point that Anita walked the phone into the bedroom where David was sleeping. She woke him and said, "It's Rory. You need to talk to him."

There is no way to cushion a blow like that one. Rory simply told his father and said he was heading to Caroline's house to try to find out what had happened.

"By the time I got there, Shey was gone," he says. "They'd taken him in an ambulance to the medical examiner's office. The cops were still there with my mom, and they said it looked to them like an overdose, but they couldn't be sure. I was pretty sure."

Rory ended up meeting his father, Anita, and Erin at the medical examiner's office. Shey couldn't be released to a funeral home until an autopsy had been performed. The autopsy confirmed what they all thought: there was alcohol in his system and a massive amount of cocaine.

"He'd built up a huge tolerance by then," Rory says. "He took a lot of it."

It is possible though that he might not have died, if not for the alcohol.

One of the first people to call Shey's father was Bill Clinton.

"There were two reasons why I called," Clinton says, remembering the conversation vividly, even five years later. "The first one, of course, was because I was so sorry. I mean, I died inside when I heard the news. There's nothing more tragic than losing a child, especially that way. I knew David would blame himself because that's what fathers do. You feel responsible for any child of yours no matter how old they are.

"But I also knew what had happened because I'd had four friends who lost children exactly that way. Too many people in our country don't understand that if you drink at all after taking an opioid you can die in your sleep. The brain stops getting the message to breathe.

"When President Obama was in office I tried to get [Arne Duncan] his secretary of education to make it mandatory that kids, young kids, be told about this and be told to make sure they passed the message to their parents to make them aware too. You just can't mix an opioid with alcohol. If you do, you're risking your life. Everyone needs to know about this. Everyone.

"He [Duncan] is a very good man, but he didn't think it was time for something like that. I'm still campaigning to try and get it done."

Clinton and Feherty talked for almost an hour—most of it was Clinton telling Feherty that even though he knew his instinct would be to blame himself, he shouldn't do that.

"He was amazing," Feherty says. "Outside of my family, his was one of the first calls. I was really in no shape to listen to anything, much less to speak, but he kept insisting I needed to listen to what he was saying and figure out a way to move on—no matter how hard that was going to be. I needed to do that for the rest of my family. I don't remember very much about those first few days, but I will never forget that call."

Feherty describes himself as "frozen" in the days following Shey's death, barely able to speak even as condolence calls and texts came in from around the world. He wasn't the only one.

"I called him and I wanted to find a way to comfort him," Sam Torrance says. "But when I opened my mouth, nothing came out—I mean nothing. I just had no idea what to say. I still don't."

Rory McIlroy had a similar experience. "I wanted so much to help because David is always there when *you* need help," he says. "I think he's the best version of himself when he's focused on others and not on himself. I called and all I could think to say over and over was, 'I'm here for whatever you need.' But that's what everyone says and, at a moment like that, there's really nothing you can do. It was heartbreaking. Still is."

It was Rory Feherty who took over in those horrific days when every moment seemed fraught with something worse than the last moment.

David remained in his "frozen" state until the family walked out of the funeral home. Then he collapsed in tears. "I don't think Erin or I had ever seen that," Rory says. "Certainly nothing like that. It was an absolutely horrible moment."

Anita Feherty still remembers her stepson's remarkable strength throughout those first few hours—and days.

"He was incredible," she says. "He just took control, did everything that had to be done because none of the rest of us could do it. I still don't know how he did it."

Rory Feherty admits he is the most stoic—his word—member of the family. He knew neither of his parents—or his stepmother or sister—were going to be able to get done what needed to be done.

"I just had to do it," he says. "Shey was always the emotional one, and I was the stoic one. Maybe it was something I taught myself growing up the way I did. It was probably more about emotional self-protection than anything else. I knew how Shey manipulated my dad for money, and I told myself I would never ask him for money. I love my dad, and I know what a good heart he has, but I never wanted to take advantage of him the way Shey did."

Erin Feherty remembers being amazed by her brother during that period. "The only thing he did that showed any stress was he started smoking again," she says. "Beyond that, he held us all together. I remember sitting there during the eulogy thinking, 'I could never do that, never.'"

"I'd completely quit," Rory Feherty says. "That day, I went and bought a pack of cigarettes. I guess that was my outlet. Shey was always troubled, but he wasn't just my brother; he was my best friend."

His sister feels the same way. "He was so much fun. All four of my brothers were wonderful to me when I was growing up. Shey was the one who would sit down and play the piano with me because he knew how much I loved it. Rory did it too, but not as often. Shey really loved doing it. He was the most playful of my brothers. I adored him."

Rory Feherty says now it wasn't until three years later that he sat down and cried about his brother's death. "I just held everything inside for a long time," he says. "I knew I couldn't break down in front of the family, especially my dad. It's a cliché, but I had to be strong. I was getting ready to deploy [to Djibouti for nine months] and I couldn't let anyone in my family think I couldn't handle what I needed to handle.

"It all stayed inside of me for three years. Then one day I came home and just broke down completely. It all came out at once."

It was Rory who gave the most touching eulogy at the funeral, finding the best that there was in his big brother.

He began by reading from something he had found in the Bible, Lamentations 3:1–19. It is a lengthy passage on dealing with loss that concludes this way: "For no one is cast off by the Lord forever. For though he brings grief he will show compassion, so great is his unfailing love. For he does not willingly bring affliction or grief to anyone."

After that, Rory spoke in his own words about his brother.

"Shey was the glue who bound a very fractured family together," he said. "He tried every day to make our lives better, not for the betterment of himself, but for his family he so desperately wanted to be happy. As I went through family photos, I couldn't help but smile because in almost every photo I saw him with his arm around someone he loved. Shey was never alone. He walked a path that none of us could follow, but in that, he accomplished an amazing feat. He brought together a family that desperately needed healing; he accomplished what he wanted most. One big happy family. Shey was my alarm clock, he was my calendar, and he was my keeper in my worst of times. When I was absorbed with anger and a callous cold heart, it was Shey who took my burdens and reminded my family how much

I really did love them. Shey was the one to remind me of birthdays, anniversaries, and important family events. It was Shey who harbored love in his heart when I didn't have enough sense to send my ships to him. Shey was the one who, no matter what circumstances he was in, always looked after my mother when I was too involved in my own life. It was Shey, who in my own worst moments, in my own worst heartbreak, sat on the floor and picked up the pieces with me.

"As of today, Shey was the one to make our family whole again.

"I will always remember my big brother as the man who had the love and the compassion to see through the hate, and love all. I will never forget my big brother."

He then introduced his mother.

"Which was a disaster," Rory says. "When I was speaking, all I was trying to get across to everyone there, but mostly to everyone in my family, was that if there was ever a time to put aside our differences and all the conflict that had gone on through the years, this was that moment. Shey had a lot of flaws, but he was the closest thing we had to glue in our family. I was hoping everyone would recognize that."

He pauses. "It took my mother about forty-five seconds—if that—to cut all that down. She trashed Shey's memory. She trashed everyone on the other side of the family. She just unloaded on my dad. It was really awful. After a while, I'm not sure people could even understand what she was saying."

The only semi-saving grace for David Feherty in that moment was that he wears hearing aids and he turned them down. Even so, he heard enough.

"She just crushed me," he says. "Everything bad that had ever happened to Shey, to Rory, but most of all to her was my fault. She just couldn't stop herself, even in that setting, even knowing that almost everyone there was from my side—my friends. My two memories of that day are Rory and all the people who came to try to comfort me in that moment."

The sad irony is that Caroline didn't need to convince David to blame himself for Shey's death. He did then; he does now. It is an understatement to say that, even though he can become *Feherty* on stage—whether that stage be TV, a theater, or a corporate outing of some kind—he is a much sadder person now than he was prior to that nightmare morning in 2017.

"I've dealt with depression, with being bipolar for a long time now. It's been diagnosed, and I take meds that help control it," he says. "But there's a part of every day when I'm just sad. Sometimes I cry; sometimes I don't. But I feel the sadness, and I know it isn't something where I can just take a pill and start to feel better.

"Any parent who has been through it can understand. It really doesn't matter how many people tell me not to feel guilty; it really doesn't matter if my shrink explains it to me. I get it intellectually, but this isn't an intellectual issue. I know all my children are genetically inclined toward addiction. I've talked to them about it. I think Rory and Erin are very conscious of making sure that they don't become me. It isn't because they don't love me, it's because they've seen up close what comes with the whole package, and they know they don't want to go down that road.

"I'm glad they get it. I want them to get it."

Rory had signed up for the National Guard as soon as he graduated from high school because, he says, he wanted to serve in the military and wanted to play a role in defending his country. But that desire—and that decision—had nothing to do with his father's involvement with the military or in Troops First or any of the events he puts on every year for those in the military and for those who are ex-military.

"Absolutely zero," Rory says in response to the question. "I liked the idea of serving my country; that was important to me. And I wanted to get into law enforcement, which I've done. But those decisions had nothing to do with my dad. I have always very much wanted to be Rory Feherty, not David Feherty's son."

And yet, when Rory thinks of his father, he has memories that make him smile. "I remember once we went dove hunting," he says. "I probably wasn't more than ten. We were sitting under a tree, and he had put his gun down next to him. I guess he hadn't locked it because, suddenly, it went off. The shot probably missed his head by a few inches.

"It could have been tragic. Instead, we just looked at each other and started laughing. Dad said, 'Jeez, that could have sucked, huh?'"

David took both Shey and Rory on road trips when he started working for CBS. "We both loved it," Rory says. "Everyone was great to us. We hung around the compound and had a great time. Neither one of us was ever really into golf, but we loved spending that time with Dad."

There was also the time when a teenage, lovesick Rory called his father looking for guidance. "I really liked this girl, and she didn't reciprocate. First love-rejected kind of thing. I called my dad and said I was really busted up about it. He didn't downplay it at all. He said, 'It's OK to cry. If you hold your emotions inside, it's like a poison. Don't feel bad about feeling sad about this.' That talk helped me deal with the whole thing so much. I've always felt when I needed him most, he would be there. I've never forgotten that talk. It meant so much to me."

Erin Feherty feels the same way about her father.

"I remember about the time I got to middle school becoming aware that he was kind of famous," she says. "And then I started noticing it when we'd go out. To be honest, I didn't love it. I saw both sides of him: the public side, which is so charming—genuinely charming. The private side isn't always that way. I've always worried about my mom, because she's always been the one who has had to handle him at his worst. Sometimes, I can't believe how strong she's been. The good news is, I think he understands that and how lucky he's been to have her."

And while both kids are often critical of their father, they also see the side of him that has made him so popular with the public.

"At times, he can be a moron," Erin says. "At other times, he's absolutely brilliant. He's so good with people who are awed just to talk to him. He makes them feel relaxed and important. I've always loved that about him.

"And he is so genuinely funny. I was really upset when I heard he was going to be doing stand-up [*Feherty Off Tour*] because I'd been telling him since I was a little kid that he should be doing a stand-up act. Someone else suggests it, and he decides to do it."

Having someone suggest he could make money doing it might have been a factor—a point Erin concedes with a laugh.

Rory has also seen both sides of his and Erin's father. "In a lot of ways, Erin's borne the brunt of a lot of things I didn't have to deal with," he says. "She was at home and saw things I never had to see. But she's right, the good side of him is *so* good.

"I watch the way he treats servers in restaurants. He treats them with as much respect as they treat him—heck, sometimes more. It makes me feel proud. I think maybe it has something to do with his background, but he's never looked at the idea that he's now famous as being something that makes him special in any way. If anything, he's a little embarrassed by it. He still sees himself as the kid who grew up in Bangor, Northern Ireland."

Erin, who *has* seen a lot more of the bad than Rory because Rory hasn't lived at home for the last dozen years, agrees. She also admits that when her father has slipped from sobriety, it scares her.

"I remember Mom telling me eight years ago that Dad was drinking again and he needed help," she says. "I think it's fair to say that I just freaked out. Honestly, I was worried about *her* [Anita]. My thought was, 'How much more can she take?' I'm not sure anyone knows how much she's been through."

It is a thought that has crossed Anita Feherty's mind more than once. Both she and David agree that the battle is far from won; it is still ongoing. They both agree there isn't a day that goes by when the thought that David might slip—or take a pratfall—crosses their minds, which is why it was so terrifying for everyone when David started to drink again after Shey's death. The reason it happened was obvious. That didn't make it any easier to deal with.

"I think Anita felt helpless," David says. "I think she felt as if she was watching me slowly kill myself. Or maybe not so slowly."

Anita knew that another trip to rehab wasn't the answer any more than it had been the answer a year earlier. She had friends call to console him and to tell him that the answer wasn't to drink himself to death. Barack Obama and George W. Bush both sent emails.

Tom Watson and Bill Clinton—two men at opposite ends of the political spectrum but who genuinely cared about Feherty—said almost the same thing to him.

"You can't bring back life," Watson says. "Everyone knows that, so you don't pretend that you can. I honestly didn't think saying, 'You'll see Shey again someday' was going to be comforting. I tried very hard to listen, to let him talk, just vent. I think he needed that. And, at some point, I told him he needed to try to move on, that he still had so many people who cared about him, loved him, needed him.

"The best thing about all that was that it was true. I wasn't making anything up. I was just telling him what I honestly thought.

"He's never going to get over it. How can you possibly get over something like that? But he has learned, I think, to live with it. Not away from it, not putting it behind him, because you can't do that either, but to live with it.

"That doesn't make it easy on any level. At best, it's hard—very hard. But he does try to live with it every day, if only for the people that he loves."

CHAPTER ELEVEN

Welcome to LIV

IT BEGAN WITH A PHONE call to Anita Feherty on a late March morning. Greg Norman knew that David Feherty rarely answered his cell phone, so he called Anita—who does answer her cell phone. The call was brief and direct: "Would you ask David to give me a call?" Norman asked.

Anita was pretty sure she knew why Norman was calling and passed the message to her husband, who quickly called Norman back. He also had a feeling he knew what the call was about, and, he admitted later, he was intrigued.

"I knew Greg was recruiting," he says. "He'd recruited a lot of players, but he was still—I suspected—looking for a splash of some kind with announcers."

There wasn't much small talk. After a couple of minutes, Norman got to the point: "I want you to come and work for LIV," he said. "I want you to be our John Madden."

Feherty's answer was instinctive: "Well," he said, "I'd have to put on at least one hundred pounds to do that."

Once the laugh had been exchanged, the two men got serious.

"I knew exactly what Greg was saying," Feherty says. "I was flattered he would think of me that way."

Putting aside the joke, trying to be John Madden in any context would be difficult. Madden had been a great NFL coach, compiling a record (including postseason) of 112–39–7 in ten seasons with the Oakland Raiders and had won a Super Bowl in January 1977.

But his greatest impact on football had come after he retired from coaching following the 1978 season at the age of forty-two. He spent the next thirty years as a broadcaster at CBS, Fox, ABC, and NBC and became one of the sport's icons in that role. His style was unique—it couldn't be copied, even though many tried—and he was universally beloved both as a broadcaster and as a person. Even though he worked late in his career with Hall-of-Fame broadcaster Al Michaels, it was his partnership with Pat Summerall at CBS and Fox that became part of football lore. They were so connected it was as if "SummerallandMadden" was one word.

Norman knew that—size aside—Feherty had Madden-esque qualities. He was universally beloved by everyone in the golf world, and he had a style that couldn't be copied. Who else in the history of golf broadcasting could possibly have come up with "Looks like an octopus falling out of a tree" to describe a golf swing—Jim Furyk's. No one enjoyed that description more than Furyk.

He had also once described Colin Montgomerie as "having a face like a warthog stung by a wasp." That, combined with the "Mrs. Doubtfire" nickname, might explain why Montgomerie was not and is not a fan.

But he might be the only one.

Feherty had never been a regular in the eighteenth tower during his twenty-five-year broadcasting career, except occasionally on

Thursday and Friday at the PGA Championship on cablecasts when several people rotated through the towers during daylong telecasts. He always knew that the eighteenth tower on network TV was reserved for past major champions, whether it be Ken Venturi, Lanny Wadkins, Nick Faldo, Johnny Miller, or Paul Azinger—all major winners he had worked with during his career.

LIV though, was different—for good and for bad. There would be no major championships on the LIV Tour; in fact, the reason for the name, the roman numeral for fifty-four, was because the tournaments would be fifty-four holes each.

LIV would look and sound more like an exhibition, more like the PGA Tour events that had once been dubbed "the Silly Season," when they were played in November and December after the real tour events of that year had been completed.

Fred Couples had so much success in those events through the years that Jack Whitaker dubbed him "Mr. November."

There would be shotgun starts on the LIV Tour, all forty-eight players in the field teeing it up at the same time around the golf course. There would be no cut, and everyone in the field would be paid at week's end. Last place money during 2022 was $120,000. There was also a team aspect each week, with four-man teams competing for additional prize money.

And there would be lots of music around the golf course. Feherty liked that idea, especially when Norman mentioned that he could be involved in selecting the music. First prize for the team event was $1.5 million, divided four ways.

At the moment that Norman first contacted Feherty, LIV was still lining up its first wave of players—offering incomprehensible amounts of guaranteed money in order to recruit stars—in addition to the mammoth purses it was offering.

That money came from the government of Saudi Arabia, although it was called "the Public Investment Fund." No one disputed where LIV's money came from or that Saudi Arabian crown prince Mohammed bin Salman was the overseer of LIV. It was bin Salman who hired Norman as the CEO of the new venture in the fall of 2021.

To say that Saudi Arabia and bin Salman were controversial figures in the world was like saying the sun plays a significant role in the existence of life on Earth.

There is almost no one on the planet who doesn't hold bin Salman responsible for the assassination of *Washington Post* reporter Jamal Khashoggi in October of 2018. Khashoggi, Saudi Arabian by birth, had been critical of bin Salman and the Saudi government, and it cost him his life in absolutely gruesome fashion.

There is also the still ongoing issue of Saudi involvement in 9/11. Fifteen of the nineteen terrorists involved in the attacks were from Saudi Arabia. In 2004, the US government–funded 9/11 commission said in its final report that it "found no evidence that the Saudi government as an institution or Senior Saudi officials individually funded [Al Qaeda] to conspire the attacks" or that it had funded the attacks.

There are still many people skeptical of that conclusion, and a later FBI report said it was "50/50" that there had been Saudi government involvement in the attacks.

Norman had taken the job working for the Saudis for two reasons: money and revenge.

In 1994, when he was the number one player in the world, Norman had attempted to start a breakaway tour, one that would have been made up of tournaments with smaller, elite fields, guaranteed money for every player, and no cut. PGA Tour commissioner Tim

Finchem was able to shut the concept down by creating a series of events called "World Golf Championships."

Each had a smaller, elite field, huge money, and no cut. It was a direct steal of Norman's concept, and it worked. Norman's new tour never got off the ground.

And Norman never forgot. Which explains why—money aside—he was willing to take another shot at running a tour that would potentially damage the PGA Tour.

With the blessing of bin Salman, Norman was able to throw huge amounts of money at players, notably Phil Mickelson, who was the first important player to agree to sign on with LIV. He was reportedly paid close to $200 million in up-front money. Norman offered closer to $800 million to Tiger Woods, still by far the biggest name and draw in golf. Woods, who is worth more than $1 billion, turned it down. Rory McIlroy also turned down money north of $100 million. Both made it clear from the beginning they had no interest in being part of LIV.

But others would follow Mickelson for huge, guaranteed money: Dustin Johnson, Bryson DeChambeau, Brooks Koepka, Sergio Garcia, Patrick Reed, Louis Oosthuizen, Charl Schwartzel, Martin Kaymer, Graeme McDowell, Henrik Stenson, Bubba Watson, and, later, Cameron Smith—who was the number two player in the world when he made the jump. All major champions, all big names in golf. Lee Westwood and Ian Poulter also joined. Neither had won a major, but they were longtime stars, especially in the Ryder Cup and especially in Europe.

It was not a coincidence that many of the players who signed on early were well past their prime. The exceptions were Koepka, Reed, DeChambeau, and Johnson. Everyone else was in their forties— except for Mickelson, who turned fifty-two in June 2022. Smith was twenty-nine when he signed on after the 2022 PGA Tour season ended in August, and Juaquin Niemann was a twenty-three-year-old rising star when he joined at the same time as Smith.

Mickelson and Stenson both gave up Ryder Cup captaincies to take the LIV millions: Stenson had already been named Europe's Ryder Cup captain for 2023. He was stripped of his captaincy— replaced by Luke Donald—soon after he announced he was moving to LIV. Mickelson had been unofficially anointed the US captain for 2025, when the matches are scheduled to be played at Bethpage Black, on Long Island. He was unofficially unanointed as soon as he pledged his loyalty to LIV.

There were other big names who turned down LIV, most notably Jack Nicklaus, who announced in May he had been offered more than $100 million to help administrate the new tour and had turned it down—twice, once verbally and once in writing. Norman, who had been a close Nicklaus friend years earlier, lashed out at him, claiming Nicklaus had supported the LIV concept when first presented with it and calling Nicklaus a "hypocrite."

Ugliness was everywhere in golf at that moment.

McIlroy never said anything about a specific offer, but he was very clear from the beginning that he had zero interest in LIV. "There's no place in golf for the LIV Tour," McIlroy said early on. He later criticized a number of players who had joined LIV, saying they had "said one thing, then done another."

One of McIlroy's close friends on tour through the years has been Garcia. They are longtime Ryder Cup teammates and were in each other's weddings. During a spring 2022 conversation about LIV, Garcia said to McIlroy, "This is our chance to get paid what we deserve."

That thinking isn't atypical for a professional athlete. Most think they "deserve" to be paid the millions they make—and more. There's nothing typical about McIlroy—perhaps because, as Feherty likes to joke, his parents dropped him on his head as a baby.

He looked at his friend that day and said, "Sergio, we're golfers. We don't *deserve* to be paid anything."

John Rahm and Collin Morikawa, two major champions in their twenties, also turned down the LIV money. Although the majority of stars fleeing to LIV early were over forty and most were well past their peaks, Mickelson had somehow won the PGA Championship in 2021, becoming the oldest man (at fifty) to win a major championship.

Johnson, who was turning thirty-eight; Koepka, who was thirty-three; Reed at thirty-two; and DeChambeau, who was twenty-nine, were the most significant exceptions and, thus, were important recruits for Norman and LIV.

Even with all these controversies swirling—some political, some financial, some athletic—Feherty was intrigued by LIV even before Norman's call. When Norman made the comment about "being our John Madden," Feherty took a step beyond intrigued.

"We only talked about ten minutes, fifteen minutes tops," he says. "But by the time I hung up the phone, I was pretty sure I wanted to do it if the money was right. And I was fairly certain the money would be right, based on what Greg had said to me."

He was comforted, he said, by the 9/11 commission's finding that the Saudi government had not been involved in 9/11. He was certainly aware of Khashoggi's death, and he knew what the term "sportswashing" meant. He also knew that sportswashing was a tactic often used by countries with repressive governments. Unlike a lot of athletes or ex-athletes, Feherty is very politically aware—whether you agree with his politics or not.

The Saudis had been involved in golf for many years, hosting a tournament on the European Tour (that moved to the Asian Tour in 2022) and paying big-name players huge appearance fees to play in their country. Woods and McIlroy had both been offered seven-figure appearance fees to appear in the Saudi tournament but had turned down the offers. After being offered $2.5 million to play in 2020, McIlroy said it just didn't feel "morally right" to play in Riyadh.

To say that sportswashing is unique to Saudi Arabia is naïve at best, hypocritical at worst. Russia hosted the Winter Olympics in 2014, and China hosted the Summer Olympics in 2008 and the Winter Olympics in 2022. The International Olympic Committee's true slogan is "Show me the money!"

The NBA has done millions of dollars of business with China in the last twenty years, and when the subject of China's repressive political activities comes up, NBA commissioner Adam Silver talks about other countries that have similar issues, which they do.

FIFA, which may be the only governing body in sports more corrupt than the International Olympic Committee, willingly sold its soul to the government of Qatar when it gave the 2022 World Cup to a country infamous for human rights violations, oppression of gays, and its worldwide involvement with Muslim terrorist groups.

A *Sunday Times* of London story in March 2019 reported that Qatar had given $880 million in bribes to FIFA officials to secure the World Cup. Even as story after story came out about countless human rights violations and the deaths of people working to build the host stadiums, FIFA didn't budge. It had been shown the money, and it wasn't giving it back.

It is almost par for the course nowadays for anyone criticized for being involved in sportswashing to point out others who are doing the same thing. LIV was no different. There was no point in denying the past only to claim that others were equally guilty or guiltier.

Ironically, it was Mickelson, in defending his decision to take the LIV money, who summed the situation up best. In an interview with biographer Alan Shipnuck in November 2021, Mickelson conceded to Shipnuck that LIV (known then as the Saudi Golf League) was sportswashing. He then went on to say: "They're scary motherfuckers to get involved with. We know they killed Khashoggi and have a horrible record on human rights. They execute people over there for being gay. Knowing all this, why would I even consider this? Because this is a once-in-a-lifetime opportunity to reshape the PGA Tour."

From there, Mickelson bashed the tour: "They've been able to get by with manipulative, coercive, strong-arm tactics because we, the players, had no recourse. As nice a guy as [Tour commissioner Jay] Monahan comes across as, unless you have leverage, he won't do what's right. And the Saudi money has finally given us that leverage. I'm not sure I even want [LIV] to succeed, but just the idea of it is allowing us to get things done with the PGA Tour."

The translation to all that is simple: it's about the money. Period. At one point when Mickelson's lawyer claimed that Mickelson's involvement was about "taking the game to places it hadn't been before while only having to play fifty-four holes each week," someone (me) pointed out that Mickelson could play exhibitions anywhere in the world he wanted to play and still play on "PGA Tour Champions"—the tour's current euphemism for the over-fifty tour—the lawyer said, "Come on, there's no real money on the Champions Tour [as it was formerly known]."

But this isn't about the money, right?

The notion that LIV is about anything other than money for those taking the Saudi money is ludicrous. Feherty knew that from the beginning and has never tried to claim otherwise.

When Shipnuck printed the excerpts from the Mickelson interview in January—as a prelude to the launch of his best-selling book, *Phil: The Rip-Roaring (and Unauthorized) Biography of Golf's Most Colorful Superstar*—it caused a sensation. Mickelson's initial response was to claim the comments were off the record.

Shipnuck has been a respected reporter in the golf world for thirty years. The idea that he would quote an explosive off-the-record comment so specifically was believed by almost no one. Even if by some chance the comments *had* been off the record, that wouldn't change their meaning. Yes, Mickelson had said, the Saudis were sportswashing. Yes, they were "murderous motherfuckers." When the "off the record" claim didn't fly, Mickelson fell back on the age-old "I was quoted out of context" cop-out.

This response reminded many in golf of the famous story of John Daly at the 1994 British Open. Daly had been quoted a week earlier in a British tabloid as saying about half the players on the PGA Tour were using performance-enhancing drugs of some kind. When Daly met with Commissioner Tim Finchem about the comments on the Monday of British Open week, Finchem asked him if he had, in fact, made them. Daly said he had, and the reporter had taped the interview.

"OK, then," Finchem said, "when it comes up, just say you were quoted out of context."

Daly followed Finchem's orders. Or at least tried to follow them.

"I was quoted out of content," he said repeatedly when the subject came up.

With or without the "out of context" cop-out, Mickelson was right about one thing: the presence of LIV could—and would—help him and other players squeeze more money from the tour.

Already, in direct response to the mere specter of LIV almost a year earlier, the tour had created something called the "Players Incentive Program" (PIP), which was a $50 million fund ($100 million in 2022) that handed out money to players based largely on their popularity on social media. Not surprisingly, Tiger Woods, who missed the last ten months of 2021 after his near-fatal car accident in February, finished first in the PIP rankings for 2021 and collected $10 million. Second on the list, collecting $6 million? Phil Mickelson. In 2022, Woods, who played nine rounds of competitive golf, finished first again, winning what was no doubt a much-needed $15 million. This time, McIlroy was second, earning an equally needed $12 million. Twenty players shared in the fund, the last five—among them Rickie Fowler, who wasn't even an exempt player—earning $2 million.

No one who had jumped to LIV was mentioned.

The tour also found more millions to boost purses considerably. All this money, according to the tour, was the result of lucrative new TV contracts that kicked in beginning in 2022.

Mickelson was also accurate when he talked about the tour withholding information from the players—and from the world in general. The tour has never opened its financial books to anyone, and it is, without question, the most secretive major sport in the United States when it comes to talking about discipline. Unlike any other professional sports organization, it never announces player fines or suspensions. Others routinely announce them, knowing that the money is rarely a deterrent, while public embarrassment can be. Former player Brad Faxon was fined once by the tour for telling the media he had been fined by the tour, in this case for saying there was no excuse for Scott Hoch skipping the British Open. Hoch didn't like links golf courses and preferred to play in a tournament in Mississippi that week, more concerned with making a buck than making history.

According to the tour, criticizing another player was "conduct unbecoming." And telling people you'd been fined? Also conduct unbecoming. Honesty is frowned on in tour world.

Feherty knew both sides of the story when Norman called. And he knew that once LIV began negotiating with his agent, Andy Elkin, the money offered would go way beyond what he was being paid by NBC. Even after *Feherty* was canceled, he was still being paid more than $1 million a year by NBC. But if the LIV money was anywhere close to what he thought it would be, he would have to give the offer serious thought.

But it wasn't *just* about the money—although that was certainly an important factor.

Feherty was restless. He had gone to NBC at the end of 2014 for considerably more money than he was being paid by CBS and because he liked the idea of moving from the ground to a tower.

"That was a mistake," he says. "When I was on the ground, I was directly involved in what was going on with the players I was following. Not just them but the caddies and everyone watching from up close. It was, for me, a lot more intimate and, I think, gave me a lot more freedom since I was looking directly at what was going on and hearing what was going on.

"It's not the same when you're on a tower, can't be the same. I thought it was time for me to move to a tower—I was almost sixty—and NBC agreed. Turned out I was wrong."

It's worth noting that announcers sitting on a tower rarely see live golf. Even when there is play on the hole right in front of them, they look at their monitor so they can see what the viewer is seeing. The view from the tower is often obstructed by the presence of several monitors. That's a lot different than standing next to a player or looking directly at a lie in the rough. Or having the most iconic figure in golf telling you dirty jokes.

Feherty never had any complaint with the way he was treated by NBC. Even though Tommy Roy, NBC's longtime golf producer, had a style that was very different from Lance Barrow's, Feherty was completely comfortable working with him.

"The difference between Tommy and Lance was simple," he says. "Lance was a TV guy who was very good at doing golf. Tommy is a golf guy who is very good at doing TV."

In all, he was welcomed at NBC with open arms. "When we first heard it was a possibility we were going to get him I think we all thought the same thing: 'Wow!'" Dan Hicks says. "He'd been with CBS for so long and was so much a part of what they did. In TV terms it was a little bit like Tom Brady leaving the Patriots to go and play in Tampa Bay. For us, it was a big deal."

Feherty had no trouble fitting in with his new colleagues. They all noticed right away that he never tried to take over the room—or a telecast. A big part of doing golf on TV is sitting around in the production trailer before a telecast, getting a feel for what's going on in the tournament and what's to be expected once the telecast begins.

"A lot of it is storytelling," Hicks says. "Everybody's got them. A lot of the time David would sit quietly, and you might think he wasn't even listening. Then, something would trigger him, and he'd tell a story, and then he'd get on a roll. Inevitably, his stories were the funniest ones anyone told."

As a Frank Chirkinian disciple, Barrow was always more concerned with telling the story of an event than with showing every possible shot. Roy has always wanted people to see *golf.* In fact, he has made it one of his goals to show at least one shot struck by each of the 156 players in the US Open. "If they're good enough to make the Open, they deserve to have their presence recorded on TV at least once," he likes to say.

Spoken like the son of a golf pro who once dreamed of playing in the US Open himself. Chirkinian's response to that notion would have been something like: "No one gives a shit about some guy who's going to be giving lessons to 20-handicappers next week."

But Barrow and Roy had one very important thing in common: both wanted their announcers to sound good and sound smart at all times. Feherty was completely comfortable working for both men.

That said, his new role was, quite unintentionally, a diminished one. Johnny Miller was NBC's longtime star as the eighteenth-hole analyst when Feherty arrived, and when Miller retired in February 2019, Paul Azinger was hired to take his spot next to Hicks on eighteen. Gary Koch, who had worked for NBC since 1996, was firmly established on the seventeenth-hole tower. From there, he also called the sixteenth hole most of the time. Roger Maltbie had been at NBC even longer, dating to 1991, and was the network's lead announcer on the ground.

"There was no way Tommy [Roy] was going to change Roger's role for anybody," Hicks says. "I loved David on the ground at CBS, but I don't think anyone's ever been better in that role than Roger."

Hicks will also point out that he's probably had dinner with Maltbie more often in the last thirty years than with his wife, ESPN's Hannah Storm. "I once said to Roger that I thought I'd had dinner with him more often than with my wife and he looked at me and said, 'You *think* you've had more dinners with me? Are you kidding?'"

Fair to say the two men are close friends.

NBC also made the unprecedented move of hiring a caddie, Jim (Bones) Mackay, who had looped for Mickelson for twenty-five years. Mackay was very good on air but missed caddying enough that he left the relatively cushy TV life to return to caddying, going to work for Justin Thomas in 2021 after four years in TV. NBC hired a second former caddie—John Wood—and he was also very good on air from day one.

All of that left Feherty working the fifteenth tower. During a major championship when all eighteen holes are televised, the holes were divided up among the announcers on towers. At the US Open at Brookline, Massachusetts, in 2022, Feherty was responsible for holes four, seven, eleven, and fifteen. Although he always had the option to open his mike at any time to make a comment, he rarely took advantage, speaking most of the time when Roy called on him to talk about play on one of his holes.

Not surprisingly, his best line of the first day was ad-libbed. NBC had showed Matthew Fitzpatrick—who would go on to win the championship on Sunday—hitting a wedge shot cross-handed. After Koch had described the shot, Feherty opened his microphone and said, "Gary, do you know why a player goes cross-handed with his wedge like Fitzpatrick just did?"

Koch, a willing straight man, said, "Why don't you tell us why, David?"

To which Feherty replied, "Because they aren't any good hitting wedges the other way."

But that sort of humor was seen and heard less and less from Feherty during his seven and a half years with NBC. Some of the reason for that was the move to the tower; some of it was social media.

"There are some things you can say that, if you're listening live and there's context, that allows people to understand you're being funny," he says. "In this day and age where almost anything can be taken out of context and splashed across social media, you can get into trouble very easily for saying something that really is innocent but ends up being portrayed as tasteless or politically incorrect in some way.

"There are things that jump into my head now that, years ago, I might have said and there would probably be no backlash at all. Now, I think, 'How will people take it if I say *this*?' and, more often than not, I just figure it's a lot easier to not say it than to say it and hope there won't be any problem with it."

No one at NBC ever told Feherty to cool his act or not to say anything about certain topics. When NBC televised the Honda Classic in February 2022, shortly after LIV became a major issue, all the announcers were told in the pre-tournament production meeting that the PGA Tour wanted them to "steer clear" of any LIV discussion. But that wasn't directed at Feherty; it was for everyone.

Just as at CBS, Feherty had a good relationship with all his on-air colleagues: Hicks, Azinger, Koch, Maltbie, and Mike Tirico, who came to NBC in 2016 and is the host for the network at major championships (and at the Players, which the tour always insists be treated as if it is a major), and on-the-ground reporters Notah Begay and John Wood.

But Shey's death took something out of Feherty emotionally that no one could bring back. And the cancellation of *Feherty* by Golf Channel was the first time since he had gone to work at CBS in 1997 that he'd had a professional setback of any kind. It also hurt personally because of all the people he had worked with on the show.

"When we taped the last show [in July 2020], we didn't know it was the last show," Feherty says. "I didn't get to say goodbye on air, and I didn't get to say goodbye to all the people I'd worked with on the show for ten years. It was very sad for me when I found out we were done.

"To this day, I'm bewildered by the decision."

Right from the start, Feherty loved doing the talk show. He took pride in going after guests who wouldn't normally be seen on Golf Channel—whether they were men who had been president or, among others, Larry David, actor Samuel L. Jackson, author James Patterson, Hall-of-Fame basketball coach Bob Knight, or Bill Russell, arguably the greatest champion in any sport and an important civil rights figure.

"That was one of my favorite shows," Feherty says of the Russell interview. "So was the Knight show. The best interviews are with smart people, and Knight, whatever else you might think of him, is smart. Russell wasn't smart; he was brilliant."

He did live shows from the Super Bowl site—regardless of which network was televising the game—and had a remarkable parade of guests. On one show, Feherty was talking to Olympic swimming superstar Michael Phelps when Michael Jordan showed up. "Not often you get two guys who are clearly the greatest in their respective sports on stage together," Feherty says, still clearly proud of the moment.

No one is completely sure why *Feherty* was canceled. The bottom line is, no doubt, the bottom line: the show was very expensive to produce. It almost always involved having an entire crew travel (frequently overseas) to the home of the interviewee and was an eight-camera shoot in order to keep it from looking like a dull, one-angle-only interview.

What's more, Feherty always taped intros and outros for each interview from a studio at Universal Studios in Orlando. Doing that involved more travel and more crew time.

Lee Trevino had been a perfect first guest. Like Feherty, he appears to be an extrovert in public but is really an introvert. At that point in his life, he was rarely doing interviews. Feherty drove from his house one day to nearby Preston Trail Country Club, where he knew Trevino spent a lot of time, found him, and asked him if he would come on his new show. Trevino agreed instantly.

The Trevino interview got terrific ratings, and so did the shows that followed. It became a badge of honor for most to be interviewed on *Feherty*.

The one truly important golfer Feherty never got on the show was Woods. "I never asked him because I knew he wouldn't be comfortable with that sort of in-depth interview," Feherty says. "I didn't want to put him in a position where he either said yes and didn't really want to do it or just said no. I figured when the day came that he wanted to do it, he knew where to find me."

The day never came. Woods has never really subjected himself to any sort of real interviews, especially since the 2009 scandal that ended his marriage. In recent years, he has cultivated a "new" image by being marginally more cooperative with the media and not stalking off and speaking to no one after bad rounds—something he did regularly when he was at his peak.

But he still doesn't take part in serious interviews that involve questions that go beyond birdies and bogeys. In fact, he's never talked about what actually happened that February morning in 2021 when he nearly died after losing control of his car en route to play in an outing in Los Angeles that was part of the massive contract he had signed with *Golf Digest*.

Once, Dan Jenkins had written a fall-down-funny "interview," with Woods in *Golf Digest* that was clearly made up that so infuriated the golfer and agent Mark Steinberg that they threatened legal action.

Nowadays, *Digest* is little more than another PR arm of Tiger Woods Inc.

If Woods had ever done a sit-down interview with Feherty, it would have been pointless if Woods had insisted on steering away from uncomfortable topics. Feherty knew that; he didn't want to do an interview that would have been full of restrictions and decided not to even ask.

Once Feherty left NBC for LIV, the possibility of a Woods interview in the future turned to dust. "Tiger is so anti-LIV he doesn't want to have anything to do with anyone connected to it," his agent, Mark Steinberg, told me in response to a request to talk to Woods about his relationship with Feherty.

The other important player who never appeared on *Feherty* was Colin Montgomerie. "I actually tried to convince him to come on dressed as Mrs. Doubtfire," Feherty says. "Would have changed his image completely. He didn't exactly embrace the idea."

After his initial telephone conversation with Norman, Feherty consulted with a handful of people about the possibility of leaving NBC for LIV: Anita; Andy Elkin, his agent; Keith Allo, who had produced all 150 *Feherty* shows; Brad Jones, his *Feherty Off Tour* promoter and manager; and Tom Watson.

No one specifically said don't do it. There were, not surprisingly, questions. Watson was concerned about him becoming part of a tour that was funded by Saudi Arabia. At one point, he sent Feherty a photo of the Twin Towers while they were ablaze with a note that said, "Something to think about."

The one who was most concerned about the possibility of leaving NBC for LIV was Elkin—even though he stood to benefit a good deal financially if Feherty went to LIV.

"It's funny, because that's what impressed me about Andy when I first met him," Feherty says. "I always say he's the un-agent. That was true in this case for sure. He wanted to be certain that I understood everything that was involved: not just the politics but leaving a place where I was doing very important events to go to a place where, at least for a while, I'd be doing events that weren't nearly as important."

It was up to Elkin to negotiate a possible deal: the money, Feherty's responsibilities, and the possibility of reviving *Feherty* in some form. There was also his NBC contract, which wasn't due to expire until the end of 2023. LIV wanted Feherty on air as soon as possible. Feherty certainly wasn't leaving NBC before the 2022 US Open and British Open had been played.

After that, the question was whether NBC was willing to let him out of the rest of his contract—which meant not doing the three PGA Tour playoff events in 2022, not doing the Presidents Cup that fall (no loss there), and missing all of 2023.

Once upon a time, NBC almost certainly would have objected to Feherty leaving early—especially when *Feherty* was still in production. But given his already diminished role and the fact that everyone at NBC liked him and understood he wanted to do this (and that the money was huge), the network was willing to allow him to leave.

"If he wanted to leave, there really wasn't much point in forcing him to stay," Hicks says. "Letting him leave was the right thing to do, and it was also the smart thing to do, under the circumstances."

"When I first heard about it, my reaction was, 'Really, he wants to do that?'" Mike Tirico says. "But when I thought about it and realized everything that was involved—including the money—my thinking was, 'Why not if this is what he wants?' I think all of us felt the same way: we'd like to see him be happy."

The deal that Elkin was finally able to make wasn't simple in any way, shape, or form. In fact, the final contract didn't get signed until Tuesday, July 19—one day *after* the story that Feherty was leaving for LIV had leaked in the *New York Post*—the leak supplied by agents representing players who had gone to LIV.

The reason Elkin went ahead with negotiations and the reason Feherty's inner circle leaned toward moving to LIV was simple: they all recognized that he wasn't especially happy with how his role—or lack of it—had evolved at NBC. Even when working major championships, he appeared bored to those around him. The only way it manifested on air was in his relative lack of humor. He still had moments, but not like in the old days. He didn't appear to have his full Feherty-ness. More often than not, he had become just another golf announcer who happened to have an Irish accent.

Allo and Feherty had become close during the ten years they had worked together on *Feherty*. Allo had grown up in Florida, the son of two music teachers, and had gone to the University of Florida thinking he would follow in their footsteps. But he'd gotten involved in radio and television production and decided to follow that path. Like Feherty, he had music in his background but had gone in a different direction as an adult.

After graduating from the University of Florida, he had ended up producing Florida football coach Steve Spurrier's coach's show for six years—convincing Spurrier to tape the show at 7:00 a.m. on Sunday mornings to make it feel less like a canned highlights show. The concept had worked. He had also worked for a while for the US Olympic Committee before landing at Golf Channel in 2007. Tom Stathakes had given him a good deal of creative independence, and that had led to, among other things, *Feherty*.

Allo's role in the show's success can't be understated. Feherty knew how to ask questions and how to be funny. Allo knew television. "Right from the beginning, I told him, 'Be half as clever,'" Allo says. "I didn't want him to go for funny all the time. If he was funny half the time, that was plenty. We didn't want the interviews to turn into David doing stand-up around the answers he was getting. He got to be absolutely brilliant at listening and following up."

Allo and Feherty had been discussing ways to bring *Feherty* back in some form when Feherty brought up the possibility of moving to LIV.

"It was at my house [in Orlando]," Allo says. "We were talking about the show and he brought up his conversation with Norman. As soon as he started talking about it, there was a part of me that said, 'He's already made up his mind.'

"I knew the negatives, so did he. But I also knew this: NBC was still paying him a lot of money, and his contract was up at the end of 2023. I thought it was possible they might not renew him or might cut back the money they were paying him. I didn't know it for sure, and I knew everyone there liked him. But network television isn't about whether people like you or not."

As it turned out, Allo was probably prescient. Late in 2022, NBC announced that both Maltbie and Koch would be "retiring," at year's end. As at CBS a few years earlier with Gary McCord and

Peter Kostis, the network had decided to go "younger." None of the four men had been looking to "retire."

Unlike Kostis and McCord, Maltbie and Koch opted to go without public objection and were treated to an on-air funeral, disguised as a "tribute," during the Father-Son tournament in December.

When Feherty heard the news about his two pals, his reaction was simple: "Boy, did I make the right decision."

During their conversation in Allo's kitchen, Feherty voiced one major concern he had to his friend. "He was used to people liking him," Allo says. "In fact, being honest, he was used to being beloved. I mean, I'd seen it up close for years: people *loved* David Feherty. He knew if he did this, there were going to be people who disliked him for doing it. Some would come back; some wouldn't. But he'd be dealing with something he'd never dealt with before in his life as a public figure."

There was also *Feherty*.

"His thought was that he would put it in the deal that they would bring the show back," Allo says. "In the end, they were talking about a *lot* of money, the kind of money that I knew was going to make it hard for him to say no, especially with the doubt that had to be there about what would happen when the NBC contract was up at the end of '23."

In the end, the whole package was impossible to say no to: millions more than NBC was paying him, with a guarantee for five years; the executive producer title; the commitment to bring *Feherty* back; and being the main guy in the eighteenth tower. Feherty had always maintained that it didn't bother him that he was never asked to work in the eighteenth tower. It is probably more accurate to say he *understood* why he was never asked to work in the eighteenth tower. Deep down he knew he would have brought a unique sensibility to the job. He just never got the chance.

It wasn't as if he didn't have moments in his work for NBC—the quip about why Fitzpatrick was hitting his wedges cross-handed was an example; his ability to identify trees, courtesy of his grandfather's teachings, being another. When Jim Furyk pushed a shot under a tree to the right of the fifteenth green on the first day of the US Open, Feherty instantly identified it as a copper maple tree.

"There aren't many I can't identify right away," he says.

But the all-out sense of humor was gone. So was a good deal of the irreverence that had made him unique and beloved in the golf world. More often than not, it just wasn't there anymore.

"Look, this is the fourth quarter of his life," Anita says. "For a long time, it didn't look as if there would be a fourth quarter, but now here it is. He went through a lot—much of it self-inflicted, no doubt, to get here. He has a right to do what's going to make him happy at this point. I could hear in his voice that first weekend [in New Jersey] a kind of enthusiasm I hadn't heard for a while. He sounded happy, and for me, that's what's most important."

Feherty agrees with his wife's assessment. "I look at this as a new beginning," he said the day before he made his LIV debut in late July 2022. "I've got a five-year contract that will take me until I'm sixty-nine. It can be a perfect way for me to go into the sunset if I want to go into the sunset then. I have no idea how I'll feel in five years, but I don't have to think about any of that for a while now."

Like most deals connected to LIV, the money involved is an astonishing amount. His NBC deal was north of $1 million a year but was only guaranteed through 2023, and Feherty knew he wanted to work beyond that. How the network would have handled a new contract is impossible to know, but there isn't much doubt that a chunk of his value had gone away with the demise of *Feherty*, regardless of how it came about or who was responsible.

Perhaps almost as important as the money was the job description. Feherty is the executive producer for LIV telecasts, meaning he has a good deal of say in the content of the telecasts—including the music. By the time he worked his second tournament, in Boston on Labor Day weekend, he was in charge of selecting the musical teases for the telecast.

He would be working on the eighteenth tower with play-by-play man Arlo White, who has done a lot of soccer but may be best known for playing himself on the hit series *Ted Lasso*.

Jerry Foltz, who also left NBC/Golf Channel—after twenty-three years there—to move to LIV, is also in the eighteenth tower, which is a boon for Feherty. Foltz, one of golf's nicest people, had been doing mostly women's tournaments in recent years and is the perfect sort of straight man for Feherty.

Foltz had become very popular with serious golf fans as the lead announcer on what is now the Korn Ferry Tour—golf's version of Triple-A baseball. As a player, Foltz had won on that tour when it was called the Nike Tour and did a superb job of relating to and understanding the pressures of playing in that atmosphere. His presence means that Feherty doesn't have to talk about every shot. Since there were no commercials during the initial five-hour streaming telecasts, having a second expert in the booth was a godsend for Feherty. The fact that he felt comfortable with Foltz on both a personal and professional level helped too.

Even so, the star of the broadcasts from the very beginning was meant to be Feherty—LIV's John Madden.

His first tournament was LIV's third. There had been tournaments in London and in Oregon before LIV, still very much in the news for reasons both good and bad, came to New Jersey in the last week of July. Eleven past major champions had joined the tour by then with a twelfth, Bubba Watson, set to announce he was signing with LIV the following week.

There were also (accurate) rumors swirling that Cameron Smith, the young Australian who had shot a stunning last-round 64 to win the British Open at St. Andrews, was also going to join the tour once the PGA Tour playoffs concluded in late August.

For LIV, that was the good.

Much of the bad stemmed from the site of that week's tournament: Trump National Golf Club in Bedminster, New Jersey. The club is a forty-seven-mile drive from Ground Zero, and many families of 9/11 victims were quite public in their objections to a tournament being played there.

It was also the club that had lost the 2022 PGA Championships in the wake of the January 6 insurrection. The championship had been played two months earlier at Southern Hills Country Club in Tulsa, Oklahoma.

Naturally, Trump continued to hold a grudge against golf's establishment for that decision and publicly threw his support to LIV whenever anyone asked—or whenever no one asked. He urged players to jump to LIV so they could "take the money." He attacked the PGA Tour and the PGA of America and insisted there was no reason to be concerned about the fact that the new tour was funded by the Saudi government.

"Nobody's gotten to the bottom of 9/11, unfortunately, and they should have," he insisted the day before the New Jersey tournament began. Once, during the 2016 presidential campaign, he had claimed that Saudi Arabia was responsible for 9/11. "Who blew up the World Trade Center?" he said during one of his many Fox TV appearances. "It wasn't the Iraqis, it was Saudi—take a look at Saudi Arabia, open the documents."

Six and a half years later, he had changed his story.

Trump was the first player to tee off in the Thursday pro-am at Trump National Golf Club and spent most of the weekend strutting around the golf course like an overweight peacock. Those working for LIV had to go through a Secret Service check to get credentialed—a routine exercise where any president or ex-president was concerned. They were also presented with a detailed memo on how they were to behave in the presence of the ex-president. The first sentence was very clear: "You will *only* address him as Mr. President."

For Feherty, the week was largely a celebration. When he first arrived at the club on Tuesday to do a routine announcers' survey of the course, he was greeted by players as a returning hero. Most couldn't wait to give him a hug and tell him how happy they were that he was on board with LIV.

"There isn't anybody in golf who doesn't love David Feherty," says Graeme McDowell, the 2010 US Open champion. "Of course, I might be a bit biased being from Northern Ireland."

It was clear throughout the week that one didn't have to be from Northern Ireland to be pleased that Feherty had joined LIV. There's only one David Feherty in golf. No other announcer could bring the sort of credibility and entertainment value he brought. Not Nick

Faldo, not Paul Azinger, not Trevor Immelman, who had been selected by CBS to replace the retiring Faldo in the eighteenth tower. Like all the other former players who had worked eighteenth-hole towers, Immelman is a past major champion—having won the Masters in 2008.

On Tuesday night, Norman hosted a dinner for LIV's TV people—announcers, producers, flaks. He gave a lengthy toast to Feherty, welcoming him as LIV's John Madden. Others joined in to pay tribute before the night was over. "I was starting to think I'd died and was witnessing my own funeral," Feherty jokes.

The next night, at a party for the players and for the pro-am participants at Gotham Restaurant in midtown Manhattan, Feherty was again received like a hero returning from overseas. "The whole thing was way over the top," he says. "The place itself was huge, and there was glitz and glamour (and Trump) everywhere. There were women walking around dressed like the Empire State building or the Chrysler Building. It was impressive, but it was also a bit much."

And then, on Friday, came his LIV broadcasting debut.

CHAPTER TWELVE

Back to the Future

THE DAY WAS GOING TO be a difficult one for Feherty, and he girded for it. He had talked throughout the week about the fact that Friday—July 29—was his son Shey's birthday. And the fifth anniversary of his death.

Shey had died on July 29, 2017, of an apparent overdose of cocaine and alcohol—dying on his twenty-ninth birthday.

Feherty's memories of that moment and the next week are still vague. Anita remembers that he simply couldn't speak for a long time. "He was in complete and total shock," she says. "He just blanked out for a few days."

Even five years later, his feelings of guilt haven't abated.

"I just wasn't there for him enough," he says. "Or for Rory for that matter. He needed me more. Rory found his own way. Shey was a sweet, gentle kid, really the sweetest boy you'll ever meet. He was one of those people everyone liked. In many ways, he was just like me."

Shey had actually been doing well for a while, working in a restaurant and moving up the ladder. "He was perfect in a job that required you to deal with people and make them like you," Feherty says. "For a while, he was in a great place in his life."

Then, somehow, Shey got it in his head that he wanted to start his own business in secondary ticket sales—the market that had been more or less cornered by StubHub and others.

"Can you imagine that career move?" David says, shaking his head, his voice becoming almost inaudible. "To this day, I don't know where he got the idea. He was naïve in so many ways—not unlike me when I was younger. Everyone begged him to keep doing what he was doing because he was doing well. His idea was doomed from the start—if not before."

Whether it was the failure of his business or other factors, things went south for Shey not long after he left the restaurant. He ended up living with his mother again, which, his father says, was bound to end badly.

David doesn't remember much about the first few days after Shey's death. Anita does. "David literally couldn't speak," she says. "His face was frozen. That's why he didn't speak at the funeral. There was no way he would have been able to begin, much less get through it. Rory more or less took over. He understood that his father simply couldn't do anything in those moments. David was in a daze."

Feherty started drinking again not long after Shey's death, usually alone, almost always trying to keep it from Anita that he was drinking again. Of course, he couldn't.

Friends and family have tried to convince him not to blame himself for Shey's death, but that's pretty much impossible. As Bill Clinton puts it, "Any father is going to blame himself when something like that happens."

The week leading up to the anniversary of Shey's death has always been difficult for Feherty. He is, generally speaking, not great at remembering dates. He honestly doesn't know how many years he worked for CBS or for NBC—among other things. I spent most of the time researching this book thinking Helen was two years older than her brother. I only learned she was three years older when I interviewed her. "I'm happy he knows when *he* was born," she said, laughing.

On June 16, the first day of the US Open, Feherty walked into the NBC compound to prepare for that day's telecast. Someone asked him how his family was doing.

"My family," he said, clearly remembering something. "Today is Erin's birthday." He looked at his watch. It was only 8:00 a.m. in Los Angeles. He sent Erin, who was turning twenty-four, a lengthy happy birthday text.

"I'm just so bad with dates," he says. "Half the time when people ask me how old I am, I have to stop and think about it." He was surprised to learn that Helen is three years older than he is, not the two he had been convinced was the truth.

But the date of Shey's birth and his death are both burned into his brain.

"Five years," he said on July 28, the day before the fifth anniversary of Shey's death and his debut on LIV television. "I once said the memory doesn't get easier, but it gets farther away. Actually, it doesn't. It's still right there in front of me. There isn't a day goes by that I don't think about him, that I don't think about what he might be doing with his life right now and what he might have become. There are moments when I just sit by myself and cry. It's such a helpless feeling. I question everything I ever did as his father.

"I know he had issues, major issues, but so did I when I was that age. If I hadn't met Anita, I probably wouldn't be here right now. He never found that person. I try not to beat myself up with guilt, but I can't help it. Shey took on a lot of the burdens of our terrible marriage when he was a kid. His mother was always telling him what a terrible father he had.

"I was away trying to play golf when he was little, and I was fighting my addictions and my demons. Both boys had to live with all that. Rory somehow figured out a way to deal with it. Shey never did. He didn't exactly have an ideal boyhood."

His voice trails off.

"Losing a child is unimaginable," says Elkin, who has twin thirteen-year-old daughters. "But for it to happen that way, to deal with the guilt I know he feels. It's just horrible."

And so, on July 29, Feherty rode to the golf course, his heart heavy with memories he couldn't escape. All morning he had been receiving texts from friends saying they were thinking about him, that they recognized how difficult the day was for him.

Well-intended, but heartbreaking. Feherty doesn't always respond to texts right away. On that morning, he answered them all.

And yet, when he arrived for work, he was all smiles for everyone, excited about the first day of the rest of his professional life.

Exactly how many people were watching that first day is impossible to know. In the United States the LIV telecasts were available only on streaming services—YouTube and Facebook. LIV press releases insisted the telecasts were available in fifty countries worldwide on free TV, premium TV, and on streaming, depending on the country. Calculating the number of viewers worldwide was impossible. In the United States, the first few tournaments averaged about one hundred thousand viewers each day.

By comparison, a network telecast on the weekend of a run-of-the-mill PGA Tour event averages a little less than two million viewers.

The last round of the US Open on NBC in June averaged more than 5.4 million viewers and the last round of the British Open—Feherty's final NBC telecast—averaged about 2.6 million viewers. Ratings for the final round of the British Open are always lower because the telecast ends before 2:00 p.m. on the East Coast and 11:00 a.m. on the West Coast.

Regardless, there was no doubt Feherty would be playing to a smaller audience on the LIV telecasts. That didn't mean the audience, or those involved with the telecast, were any less adoring.

The open of Friday's telecast was all about Feherty: players welcoming him on camera, talking about what his presence would mean to LIV. Phil Mickelson had been in Rwanda prior to the event, and LIV paid to send a camera crew to tape a five-second hit with him welcoming Feherty—a gorilla in the background.

When Mickelson stepped up to hit his opening tee shot a few minutes later, Feherty quipped, "The gorilla whisperer."

He had other Feherty moments, but he was careful not to go overboard because he wanted to be sure those watching knew he was taking the tournament seriously. "I was looking for a balance between having fun with it and making sure I was treating it the way I'd treat any golf tournament that isn't one of the four majors," he says. "I think as time goes by, I'll go further with the humor, but I really did feel more comfortable than I had in a long time. It was good to get the first one under my belt."

He did get off one line that surely would have gotten him banned at Augusta when he described trying to get a golf ball onto the tiny seventh green as "like trying to hit a Pygmy's nipple."

Imagine how that line would have played with the green jackets.

On Sunday morning, Feherty noticed a handful of protesters outside the front door of his hotel. They were from a group of families of 9/11 victims that had been urging LIV—to no avail—not to play at a Trump-owned golf course. Feherty walked outside to talk to them.

"They weren't hostile or rabid or angry," he says. "They have strong feelings about what happened, and who can blame them? I think they want people to understand why they're still upset, and I listened. I think I came away understanding their point of view."

The telecasts had only one serious glitch. On Sunday, during the opening sequence, White turned to ask Feherty a softball first question. As Feherty started to answer, he realized that the Adderall tablet he had just taken was stuck in his throat.

Given that he couldn't speak at that moment, Feherty had only one choice: he coughed the Adderall up, caught it in his mouth, and then swallowed it again.

"Inauspicious start to the day," he says, laughing. "That was a new one, a first, and, I hope, a last. It will give me something to talk about down the road, I suppose."

The three telecasts that weekend were very much lengthy LIV infomercials, as one might expect. White went on and on about how thrilling the team aspect of the new tour was, and Feherty and Foltz talked about how warm the atmosphere had been around the golf course all week.

"You know one thing the shotgun start does is put everyone in the locker room at the same time," Feherty said at the start of Friday's telecast. "They all tee off at the same time and they finish at the same time. That means they see more of one another since the starting times aren't staggered from early morning until afternoon. I think that makes for more camaraderie among the players. You can feel it."

The fact that most of them already had huge amounts of guaranteed money in their pockets before they teed it up probably didn't hurt either.

The prize money was certainly mentioned: $4 million to the winner after the conclusion of the fifty-four-hole tournament; down to $120,000 for last place; and another $3 million to be divided up at week's end by the winning four-man team.

Feherty's first winner's check as a professional, £5.00, or US$7.50, for winning the Ladies Tankard Pro-Am in Belfast, was also mentioned.

The day before the New Jersey tournament began, Norman announced that there would be fourteen tournaments worldwide in 2023, and each would include twelve four-man teams in addition to the individual competition. Projected prize money for the year: $405 million.

Naturally, there was no on-air discussion about *where* that money was coming from. Everyone watching knew anyway.

Perhaps by coincidence—perhaps not—the PGA Tour announced the day after the New Jersey LIV event concluded that it would dole out $415 million in official prize money during its 2022–23 season. Of course, that money would come from forty-seven official seventy-two-hole events. A *lot* of money, just not LIV money.

Three weeks later at a players-only meeting called by Tiger Woods and Rory McIlroy, at the second PGA Tour playoff event in Wilmington, Delaware, a new plan was proposed to a small group of star players. The meeting was a big enough deal that Woods, who wasn't playing, flew in for it.

Not surprisingly, the main thrust of the new proposal that came out of the meeting was money. The tour would be broken into two distinct tournament groups: there would be twenty "elevated" events played for massive money—at least $20 million in purses for each tournament and, in many cases, more than that.

That grouping would include the four majors; the three playoff events; three tournaments "hosted" by superstars—Tiger Woods, Jack Nicklaus, and the family of the late Arnold Palmer; the Players Championship; the Match Play Championship; the Tournament of Champions (which would be expanded to include non-champions); and two international events. Other events in the category were chosen in the fall based on whether sponsors were willing to pony up more money to be included. The four events added in the fall were Phoenix (sponsor Waste Management), Hilton Head (sponsor RBC), Charlotte (sponsor Wells Fargo), and Hartford (sponsor Travelers Insurance).

Players would agree to commit to a minimum of twenty tournaments—as opposed to fifteen in the past—in return for the massive pay raise.

The elevated non-majors would have fields of sixty players, no cuts, and guaranteed money for everyone teeing it up. If that sounds a lot like a field of forty-eight players, no cuts, and guaranteed money it is because it *is* almost identical.

The rest of the PGA Tour would continue to be made up of the weekly events from the Sony Open in Hawaii in January to the Wyndham Championship in Greensboro in August. The question was this: Would title sponsors still be willing to pony up a fee that was generally around $12 million for fields not likely to have much star power, if any at all? By late fall, Honda, the tour's longest-running corporate sponsor (forty-two years) had announced that

2023 would be its last year as a title sponsor. There was, no doubt, more to come.

Every fully exempt tour player would receive $500,000 up front each year, a far cry from the $100 million being paid to a handful of LIV players, but the first time the tour had ever sanctioned guaranteed money just for being on tour. Plus, any player who missed a cut would receive $5,000 in expenses for the week. The days when Saturday and Sunday were known as the "cash rounds" on tour would be officially gone.

There was also an expansion of the so-called PIP—Players Incentive Program—which would go from $50 million divided among ten players to $100 million handed out to twenty players at year's end in 2022. The tour claimed that social media presence would no longer be a factor in "ranking" the players but would be replaced by an "awareness criteria," whatever the heck that meant.

When PGA Tour commissioner Jay Monahan announced the changes at his annual "state-of-the-tour" press conference in late August at the Tour Championship in Atlanta, he also announced a series of interactive team events, to be held on Monday nights beginning in January, that would be backed by a group that included Woods and McIlroy.

Hearing about the no-cut, elite field events, the elevated prize money, and the team events, Greg Norman couldn't resist an Instagram meme. Beneath side-by-side photos of himself and Monahan he wrote:

Jay: "Hey, can I copy your homework?" Greg: "Sure just make it look different so it doesn't look to obvious."

Whoever typed the meme didn't know the difference between *too* and *to*, but it was still a scathing—and accurate—assessment.

Alan Shipnuck, the author who had first quoted Mickelson on his reasons for taking on the tour by jumping to LIV sent out a three-word tweet: "Phil was right."

Feherty was nowhere near any of the three playoff events since he was no longer working for NBC. He was on his farm, relaxing, getting ready for his second LIV event in Boston. He was amused—and a little bit bemused—by what was going on in his absence.

"It's almost a carbon copy if you think about it," he said, talking about the changes announced by Monahan. "I think it's clear none of this happens without LIV. Whatever you might want to say about LIV, you can't say it hasn't been good for golfers. The tour and everyone who is pro-tour has been screaming from the beginning about how guarantees would take away motivation for players. Well, now they've got guarantees. The best players aren't motivated by money anyway. Nicklaus? Woods? Did they like making money? Sure. But did they play for the money? No, they played for history.

"Whatever else anyone might want to say about Phil, he certainly had it right when he said LIV would create leverage that hadn't been there before."

Feherty hadn't been aware of the Norman meme. He laughed hearing it. "That's Greg," he says. "He's also right."

And the Monday-night teams events? "Maybe they can get the Manning brothers to do their own telecast," he says, referencing the telecasts that Peyton and Eli Manning do during Monday Night Football games that are so much more entertaining than the actual play-by-play telecast.

Feherty had been comfortable sitting out the three playoff events—until the weekend in Atlanta. "I'm not a fan of the system," he says. "I mean starting guys out with an advantage like they do makes it less competitive. I would think you would want your last tournament to be the *most* competitive you can make it, not less competitive."

But when Rory McIlroy came roaring from behind on Sunday to make up a six-stroke deficit and beat Scottie Scheffler by one stroke to win the tournament and the $18 million FedEx Cup bonus, Feherty got caught up in it.

For the record, McIlroy beat Scheffler by seven shots for the week, and Scheffler, who technically finished second and received $6.5 million, had the twelfth-best score for the four days at East Lake in Atlanta among the twenty-nine players in the field. But the silly system created by the tour that allowed Scheffler—as the FedEx Cup points leader going into the event—to start with a two-shot lead on points runner-up Patrick Cantlay and up to ten shots on the last players to make the field, allowed him to hang on for second place in the final standings.

Even so, Feherty got caught up in what he was watching on Sunday.

"I really had serious twinges when Rory got into contention," Feherty says. "I loved what he was doing, especially after St. Andrews [the British Open] where he just couldn't make a putt on Sunday. That had been heartbreaking for me to watch. This was thrilling. I really did wish I was there."

Feherty had never said an actual goodbye to his NBC colleagues at St. Andrews because he was under strict orders from Elkin to not talk about the LIV deal until the contract was actually signed. On Monday morning, after Atlanta, his on-air colleagues and Tommy Roy got a group text from Feherty:

"Boys, what a great finish to a great season," it said. "I'm only sorry I couldn't be there to finish it with you. Love, df."

"I think it meant a lot to all of us," Hicks says. "Typical David. Simple. Heartfelt. I know that everyone responded. We all miss him."

Feherty was quite comfortable working with White and Foltz, although five hours as the main focus of the telecast with no commercial breaks was clearly exhausting. He stayed upbeat throughout, though, and, at the end of the day when White asked him how he felt about his first day with the new tour, he said, "I loved it. I can't stop grinning."

He was grinning through his tears, which is what he has done for most of his life.

"Actually, working that day was the best thing for me," he says. "There was no way I wasn't going to be thinking about Shey, but being on air forced me to focus on the golf. Tired as I was, six hours would have been just fine with me instead of five.

"I've always done better in my life when I'm doing something. During my first marriage, traveling and playing golf—and alcohol and drugs—were my escape from the pain. Now, working, whether it's television, stand-up, or speaking, is my escape from the pain of Shey's death."

Surprisingly—or, perhaps not surprisingly given the way most people feel about him—there was limited public blowback to Feherty's decision to move to LIV. He lost one job—his once-a-week SiriusXM show with Gary McCord that aired on Sirius's PGA Tour channel. He missed working with McCord, but the $1,000 a week he was being paid wasn't going to break his bank account.

The only national columnist who really went after Feherty was Phil Mushnick, the *New York Post*'s brilliantly acerbic media columnist. Mushnick had read the statement put out by LIV under Feherty's name along with the announcement.

The statement was clearly written by a LIV PR person.

"As a storyteller this is a one-of-a-kind opportunity to help write a new chapter in this sport's history," it said. "LIV Golf is developing ideas and innovations that are going to grow the audience and engage the next generation of players and fans.

"I'm excited by the energy LIV Golf is creating and I'm eager to contribute to a world class broadcast that has a vision toward the future."

That sounded about as much like Feherty as Tiger Woods sounded like Arnold Palmer. Maybe less. But that was the spin LIV wanted from all their very wealthy new employees.

The week after his debut in New Jersey, Feherty attended a charity event in Toledo along with Gary Koch. During the Q+A, *Toledo Blade* columnist David Briggs asked Feherty about why he'd jumped to LIV.

This time, the answer came from Feherty, not from a press release.

"Money," he answered. "People don't talk about it. I hear, well, it's to grow the game. Bullshit. They paid me a lot of money."

Mushnick had taken umbrage in his column, noting the juxtaposition of this "fit of candor" in light of Feherty's decision to become an American citizen in 2010, as well as his support of US troops.

The issues, other than money, that led to Feherty's LIV decision were arguably almost as significant: getting to be the main guy on the eighteenth tower, bringing *Feherty* back, his input as an executive producer, and the contract being for five years. But the bottom line was the bottom line: money. Feherty wasn't going to pretend that wasn't the case.

"None of us know what's going to happen," he says. "But Greg's been able to recruit some very good players and there's no doubt the PGA Tour has noticed. I hope at some point something will be worked out so the best guys can play against the best guys."

Feherty rarely uses social media in any form. Although he has almost seven hundred thousand Twitter followers, he hardly ever tweets, and when he does, it is usually about one of his charity events. Someone did send him the Mushnick column. The only thing that bothered him was Mushnick questioning his patriotism.

"I know who I am, and I know how I feel about my country," he says. "I've raised more than $30 million in twenty years for people connected to the military. I shouldn't have to defend my record on any of that."

Feherty's future—at least for the next four years—appears to be pretty clear. He will travel the world working for LIV. He will continue to do *Feherty Off Tour* and corporate speaking. He will bring *Feherty* back, albeit in a different format. He will continue to raise money for those who are serving or have served in the military. He will continue to make people laugh in public and in private.

And he and those who love him will "white-knuckle" it, hoping he can fight off his demons and his past and stay sober. It is an all-day, every-day challenge.

EPILOGUE

How do you sum up a life like David Feherty's? You don't, because it is too complicated to be described in a couple of sentences or paragraphs or perhaps even in a book. What's more, it is still evolving. He will turn sixty-five on August 13, 2023, and presumably there's a lot more of his story still to be written.

There is a story that his older sister, Helen, tells that might give some insight into the circuitous journey of a baby whose father put the wrong name on his birth certificate to a figure as recognizable as any in golf this side of Tiger Woods.

The first time Helen came from Northern Ireland to visit David during a tournament weekend several years after he had started to work for CBS, she was walking inside the ropes with him as he followed the final group.

"A number of people asked me who I was and why was I inside the ropes," she remembers. "Not in any sort of rude way, more out of curiosity. Clearly, I wasn't doing anything and yet there I was. When I explained that I was David's sister, they were all very impressed and started telling me how much they enjoyed and liked him.

"After a while, David was able to come over and say hello to some of them. The looks on their faces made it so clear how big a deal it was for them to meet *David Feherty*. It was quite a revelation for me.

I knew he'd done well on television, and we were often able to see the telecasts at home, but I really hadn't understood what a star he'd become. I remember thinking, 'I guess he's come a long way from being my occasionally annoying little brother to where he is now. Or, more importantly, I supposed, *who* he is now.'"

There's little doubt that if you took Feherty's story to Hollywood and proposed it as a work of fiction you'd be kicked to the curb pretty quickly. He went from a middle-class kid growing up during the Troubles in Northern Ireland to a teenager who dropped out of high school and chose chasing a career in golf over a career as a singer.

He was, at best, a long shot to make it as anything more than a club pro giving lessons to 20-handicappers. Instead, he became an excellent player on the European Tour and a part of what was arguably the most famous Ryder Cup ever played. In the singles that historic weekend, he hit the shot of his life to beat a future Hall of Famer.

Wait, there's more.

After playing his entire career as a functioning alcoholic who also had drug addiction issues, he went through a horrific divorce but somehow stumbled into meeting and marrying the woman of his dreams even after showing up falling-down drunk on their first date.

When he could no longer play golf well enough to make a living, he found television—or, more accurately, television found him. He became a star because he was like no one else who had ever been handed a microphone during a professional golf tournament—on either side of the Atlantic Ocean.

"I mean, who else comes up with 'That's going to run more than the nose of a toddler with a cold?'" his former NBC colleague Dan Hicks asks rhetorically.

Who else comes up with "Mrs. Doubtfire" for Colin Montgomerie or calls Rory McIlroy "Scunger," an Irish term for someone who can't play golf, and—in McIlroy's case—remains his close friend?

Let's walk through the list of ex-golfers who end up hosting an interview show on Golf Channel and interviewing *four* presidents on that show? Not presidents of golf clubs, presidents of the United States. Here's the list: Feherty.

The first check he ever cashed as a professional golfer was for $7.50. Forty-three years later, he signed a contract for millions and millions more over the next five years.

Not bad for a kid who grew up in a 1,200-square-foot home in Bangor, Northern Ireland, and shared a bedroom with his younger sister as a kid.

He's been to rehab—where he flunked himself out after twelve days, went to the airport, and had four drinks before he got on a plane to fly home. He's been to Alcoholics Anonymous meetings and has used bike riding and shooting at targets as his version of AA.

"An addict needs something to feed his addiction," his wife, Anita, says. "As long as it isn't alcohol or drugs, I'm fine with whatever works for him."

He's fallen off the wagon and climbed back on so many times he long ago lost count. He believes in both his ability to get drunk and stay drunk and his ability to get sober again. But he readily admits, "I white-knuckle every day trying to stay sober."

He has lived a dream life—as Helen points out when wondering at her little brother's remarkable fame—and his life has also been a nightmare.

His first marriage was, as he puts it, "a nonstop hostage situation." He's fought his addictions for as long as he can remember.

And he suffered life's most horrific tragedy when his son Shey died of a drug overdose at the age of twenty-nine.

Shey is the only subject that softens his voice so much his words can be hard to hear, literally and figuratively.

There is no way to not be changed forever by losing a child. Feherty certainly gives his best effort. He has the unique ability to make an audience laugh so hard that many are moved to tears. None can truly understand that someone so funny spends at least part of every day in tears—even with all the meds he takes.

"Depression is when sadness becomes hopelessness," he says often.

There is nothing sadder or more hopeless than the loss of a child.

He is beyond proud of his other two children—Rory, Shey's younger brother, and Erin, who is the daughter he and Anita had in 1998. And yet, both of them say that the man who can walk onstage and do almost two hours of stand-up comedy off the top of his head often has trouble telling them how he feels.

"I remember going out to the farm with my fiancée for a couple of days to visit him," Rory says. "It was very pleasant. After she left, Dad said to me, 'You know I really like her.' Honestly, I'm not sure the two of them spoke five sentences to one another the entire time she was there. He wasn't being unfriendly; he's just a lot more introverted than people think."

Indeed, Feherty is very much an introvert, although the fans who flock to him in public places would never know it. He talks often about how his father, who died of Alzheimer's disease in 2016 at the age of ninety-one, was one of those people who was "best friends to everyone he ever met."

Billy Feherty's son isn't that way, but those who ask for selfies or ask for an autograph or have a story they *must* tell him would never know that. They all walk away thinking they've just made a new BFF.

In researching this book, I asked everyone I spoke to about Feherty how they would describe him to an audience of people who had no idea who he was. Two words came up in every answer: *funny*—no surprise there—and *kind*. There is a generosity of spirit that is often hidden by the acerbic wit but becomes apparent to anyone who spends any time at all with him.

"I would first of all say, 'get comfortable,' because you're going to be here awhile," Mike Tirico says. "And then I'd say, be ready to laugh a lot and, finally, walk away feeling like you've made a friend for life—because you probably have."

Feherty's justifiably proud of all the money he's raised (more than $30 million) through his Troops First Foundation, and he loves the time he has spent with military and former members of the military. He says his proudest day was February 23, 2010, when he formally became an American citizen with several dozen of his friends from the military there to cheer him on.

Two years later, the Department of the Army awarded him the Outstanding Civilian Service Award for his work with Troops First.

He may be just as proud of the fact that his high school, Bangor Grammar, invited him back to be the commencement speaker. "I guess they forgot I never graduated," he likes to say with a laugh. He resisted the urge during his speech to call out some of the teachers he disliked—although he remembers them all quite distinctly.

In August 2018, I had dinner in Philadelphia with Feherty and McIlroy. The subject turned to that year's Ryder Cup—which was a few weeks away.

"It's just three of us in this room," I said to Feherty. "Tell me honestly who you want to see win."

He was sitting next to McIlroy, who would be playing in his fifth Ryder Cup for Europe. The two men had grown up five miles apart (in different eras) in Northern Ireland.

Feherty answered without even a moment of thought. "I'm an American," he said. "I want to see the Americans win."

McIlroy smiled. "Will you at least root for me to win my matches?" he asked.

"Only if they don't decide the outcome," Feherty said.

"Let me be sure I have this straight," I said. "You grew up in Northern Ireland. You *played* for Europe in the Ryder Cup, and now you root *against* the team you once played for?"

"Ardently," Feherty said.

McIlroy and I looked at one another. "You surprised?" I asked him. "Disappointed?"

McIlroy shrugged. "Neither," he said. "Let's face it, there's no one like David. He's the one and only and that's why so many people love him. Me included."

Enough said.

ACKNOWLEDGMENTS

It is easy to know where to start in thanking the people who made this book possible: David Feherty.

Also, David Feherty and David Feherty.

David and I had talked for a long time about my writing a book on his remarkable life, and yet I was surprised when I brought it up in March 2021 and he said, "It's time. Let's do it."

I was honored—and I'm still honored—that he trusted me to tell his story, which is so full of twists and turns, there were moments when I felt almost dizzy as I wrote. Of course, it is those twists and turns that make his life so remarkable. For all the pain he has suffered for so many years, he's still managed to touch an amazing number of lives.

He could not have been more generous with his time or more patient with my questions. Never once did he roll his eyes and say, "Haven't we been through this before?" even though the answer would have been yes.

Almost as important, he asked his family members not only to speak to me but to do so candidly. I never felt as if anyone pulled a punch. It will be apparent reading this book how extraordinary Anita Feherty is (also truly patient both with her husband and, in a different context, with me).

But I'm also grateful to David's children Rory and Erin and to his mom, Vi, and older sister, Helen—who straightened me out when I mentioned that she was two years older than David. "Three years," she said. When I repeated this to David he said, "Oh, really? Glad one of us remembered it right."

Others who have been important in David's life were also beyond helpful: David Jones, his first boss and mentor, and Sam Torrance, his best friend, who might be the funniest person I've ever interviewed if not for David (and the late Jim Valvano). There's also Tom Watson, who has helped keep David alive and, as Anita puts it, "between the yellow lines of life."

Rory McIlroy has been wonderfully open and available to me on several books now and this was no exception. He gave me all the time I could have asked for and was his usual honest and very smart self.

There's more: Lance Barrow, David's boss at CBS, and Ted Shaker, who was responsible—along with Lance and the late Frank Chirkinian—for hiring David for his first TV job. His on-air colleagues at CBS: Gary McCord, Jim Nantz, and Bobby Clampett. At NBC, his boss Tommy Roy and colleagues Dan Hicks, Jimmy Roberts, Gary Koch, Mike Tirico, and Mike Harper. At Golf Channel, Tom Stathakes, who played a major role in coming up with the idea for *Feherty*.

Also at Golf Channel, Keith Allo, who produced all 150 *Feherty* shows and will produce the new version of the show for LIV. And special thanks to Courtney Holt, who has been Golf Channel's MVP for years, played a key role in booking guests for *Feherty*, and helped me track down quite a few people I needed to talk to for this book.

Thanks also to David's agent, Andy Elkin, who had some understandable concerns about a book in which David would speak candidly about his life but listened openly to the idea and then was very helpful throughout the process.

I was very fortunate that Michael Pietsch, my longtime editor at Little, Brown, is now the CEO at Hachette Book Group USA. It was Michael who put me in touch with Brant Rumble at Hachette, who was the perfect editor for this book and for my many quirks. Thanks also to my longtime agent Esther Newberg, who represented me on forty-six books. As she pointed out, that's a pretty good run. Also to ICM's longtime lawyer, John Delaney, and Esther's assistant, Estie Berkowitz.

Thanks, as always, to many friends: Keith and Barbie Drum; Jackson Diehl and Jean Halperin. Jackson just retired after a remarkable forty-four-year run at the *Washington Post*. Also Frank Mastrandrea; Chris Ryan (whose phone message still has Feherty's voice on it); Bob Woodward, Elsa Walsh, David Maraniss, Tate Armstrong, Mark Alarie, and Jay Bilas (yes, all Duke guys); Gary Williams and Steve Bisciotti (*not* Duke guys); Wes Seeley, Tony Kornheiser, Mike Wilbon, Mike Sanders, David Sanders, Pete Teeley, Vivian Goldstein, Bob Zurfluh, Larry Dorman, Robby Robinson, Terry Hanson and Patti Hanson, and Andy Dolich. Major thanks to my longtime pal Mary Carillo. And to my few remaining friends in tennis: Patrick McEnroe and Mark Preston.

Special thoughts go out to longtime *USA Today* golf writer Steve DiMeglio as he battles cancer with courage and humor.

Other golf people who are important to me: David Fay, Mike Davis, Mary Lopuszynski, Marty Caffey—who has been putting up with me now for *thirty* years—Paul Goydos, Billy Andrade, Jeff Sluman, Davis Love III, Neil Oxman, Frank Nobilo, Brandel Chamblee, Lee Patterson, Mike O'Malley, Mike Purkey, David Duval, Rich Lerner, Ken Kennerly, Steve Flesch, Bill Leahey, Andy North, Drew Miceli, Brian Henninger, Lisa Cornwell, Gary Williams, Kristi Setaro, Jeremy Davis, Todd Lewis, Frank and Jaymie Bussey, Sid Wilson, Henry Hughes, Guy Scheipers, and Dave Lancer. Also Bruce Edwards's family: Jay, Chris, and Chris's husband, John Cutcher. And Gwyn Dieterlie and Len Dieterlie.

Rules guys, emeritus and current: the great duo of Mark Russell (and his family, Laura and Alex) and Slugger White, Jon Brendle, Steve Rintoul, Robbie Ware, Dillard Pruitt, and Jon Paramour.

Colleagues at the *Washington Post*: Matt Vita, Matt Rennie, Matt Bonesteel, Sally Jenkins, Marty Weil, Mark Maske, Gene Wang, Micah Pollack, and Kathy Orton. Special thanks to my editor Dan Steinberg, who somehow never loses his sense of humor even when I'm railing at him. And, of course, Posties emeritus Lexie Verdon, Steve Barr, and Sandy Boodman.

There are lots of other friends I need to mention: Ed Brennan, my old swim coach, who convinced me to give up a certain NBA career to become a swimmer. All swimming for Ed did for me was get me into college and, years later, save my life. When the doctor told me almost fourteen years ago that I had seven blockages in my arteries, I said, "Impossible. I swim four days a week. I feel fine." He said, "You're alive because you swim. Your heart is so strong it's been overcoming the blockages." Thanks, Ed.

The doctors who saved my life back then were Joe Vassallo, Lowell Sattler, and Steve Boyce, who was willing to operate on me even though I am—his words—"a fucking Duke guy." Steve's an angry (but brilliant) Maryland guy.

Bob DeStefano, whom I first met at fourteen and has been a mentor to me since then.

Basketball people: Lefty Driesell, as sharp now at ninety-one as ever. Mike and Mickie Krzyzewski; Roy Williams; Tony Bennett; Seth and Brad Greenberg; Dan Bonner—still the most underrated hoops analyst ever—Tom Brennan; Jim Calhoun; Steve Donahue; Phil Martelli; Billy Lange; Mike Brey; Bobby Cremins; the Odoms: Dave, Lynne, Ryan, and Lucia; Pat Skerry; Pat Flannery; Zach Spiker; Tom Brennan; Matt Langel; Nathan Davis; Ed DeChellis; Emmett Davis; Mike Rhoades; Ed McLaughlin; Robby Robinson; Jimmy Allen; Griff Aldrich; Tim Hall; Chris Caputo; Rick Barnes; Kim English; Chris Knoche; Ed Tapscott; Gordon Austin; and Mike Werteen. And, of course, Hoops and Joanie Weiss.

The sport will greatly miss Krzyzewski, Jay Wright, and Fran O'Hanlon. But at least it is getting Fran Dunphy back. That is a bonus for all of us.

Basketball lost one of its great men, Tom Konchalski, when Tom lost his battle with cancer two years ago. I dedicated a book to Tom and to Frank Sullivan—"the only two honest men in the gym"—several years back. The highlight of any trip to Boston for me is seeing Frank and Susan Sullivan.

Not done yet: Rick Brewer, Steve Kirschner, Lesley Visser, Pete Van Poppel, Gary Cohen, Pete Alfano, Andrew Thompson, Jim Cantelupe, Derek Klein, Dicky Hall, Tim Kelly, Eddie McDevitt, Bob Arciero, Gus Mazzocca, Anthony and Kristen Noto, Phil Hoffmann, Joe Speed, Dean and Ann Taylor, Bob Beretta, Rich DeMarco, Joe Beckerle, Dean Darling, and Tony Marino.

I will always be grateful to everyone at Navy for welcoming me back: Ken Niumatalolo, Chet Gladchuk, Eric Ruden, and Scott Strasemeier. Thanks also to Boo Corrigan for eight great years at Army.

Tim Maloney, a friend since I covered his first political campaign in 1978. Tim and I have lost our two favorite elected officials, Governor Harry Hughes and Attorney General Steve Sachs, in the last couple of years. We miss them both greatly. Thanks to Governor Hughes, I *am* an admiral of the Chesapeake Bay, dating to 1983.

Also: Harry Kantarian, Bob Edwards, Tom and Jane Goldman, Holland and Jill Mickle, Bob Costas, and my former radio colleagues: Andrew (Arnold) Bogusch, Pete Bellotti, and Max Herman.

Swimming friends, in the hope we get the KH gang back together in a pool and in a bar soon: Jeff Roddin, Jason Crist, Wally Dicks, Clay F. Britt, Mark Pugliese, Paul Doremus, Mike Fell, Danny Pick, Erik, Dr. Post Osbourne, John Craig, Doug Chestnut, Penny Bates, Carole Kammel, Peter Ward, Tom Denes, A.J. Block, Mary Dowling, and Peter Lawler.

The Red Auerbach lunch group lives even with many different faces: Aubre Jones, Murray Lieberman, Lew Flashenberg, Steve Polakoff, Stanley Copeland, Jeff Gemunder, Geoff Kaplan, Mark Hughes, Harry Huang, and, in absentia, Jack Kvancz, Pete Dowling, and Bob Campbell. We still miss Red, Zang, Hymie, Reed, Rob, Arnie, and Morgan.

Last, but never least, my sister, Margaret, and her sons, Ethan and Ben; my brother Bobby, his wife, Jennifer, and their sons,

Matthew and Brian. Also my in-laws, Marlynne and Cheryl. And, more than ever, my ever-patient wife, Christine, and my three spectacular children, Danny, Brigid, and Jane. I love them all dearly.

—John Feinstein,
Potomac, Maryland,
October 31, 2022

INDEX